History of the Church

A Captivating Guide to the History of the Christian Church and Events Such as the Crusades, Missionary Journeys of Paul, Conversion of Constantine, and Reformation

Free Bonus from Captivating History
(Available for a Limited time)

Hi History Lovers!

Now you have a chance to join our exclusive history list so you can get your first history ebook for free as well as discounts and a potential to get more history books for free! Simply visit the link below to join.

Captivatinghistory.com/ebook

Also, make sure to follow us on Facebook, Twitter and Youtube by searching for Captivating History.

Contents

Part 1: Church History

A Captivating Guide to the History of the Christian Church, Including Events of the Crusades, the Missionary Journeys of Paul, the Conversion of Constantine, and More

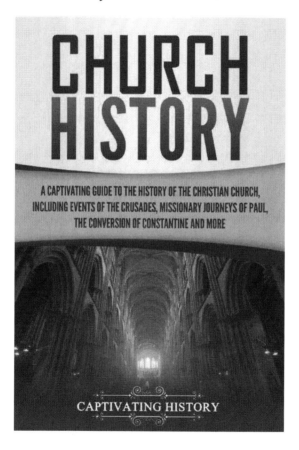

Introduction

The history of the Christian Church is a complex tale of theological disputes, liturgical controversies over the form of worship, and organizational intrigues. It is the story of the evolution of thought, practices of worship, and the formation of institutions directed toward the goal of preserving, disseminating, and interpreting the teachings of Jesus Christ, his followers, and Jewish history and texts that forecast the appearance of the Christian Messiah.

The Christian Church evolved from its early disorganized form into a highly structured social institution. It formed a focus for civilization around which social norms were established, and it became the primary institution that framed human interaction, establishing the calendar for human activities and festivities and eventually standing at the apex of human obligations of one social class to another. Despite claims of adherents coming from all walks of life, the church was never a singularity. Even at the height of its power, it was not an ecclesiastical monolith nor a singular force in the evolution of the secular world's culture. Right from the beginning, different practices and different interpretations of the Holy Scriptures produced contending beliefs, which often led to schismatic churches. The continual fracturing of the institution of the Christian Church throughout its history is as much owing to the human propensity to obtain power as it is to the finer points of theological concepts regarding Christ's historical life, the Trinity, and God's purpose for His creation.

What forms the history of the Christian Church is a convoluted and seemingly perpetual series of dialogues, discourses, and disputations among the faithful, which often descended into serious, often violent, wrangling over the meaning of every term in what one might assume was the straightforward definition of Christianity, a religion based on the person and teachings of Jesus of Nazareth. This quarreling over theological matters, particularly over what Christ said and how it is to be understood, has evolved in concert with the evolution of society. Thus, the religious practices and beliefs of Christians in the Roman Empire are distinct, for example, from those of modern-day Cuban Santeria, a fusion of Catholic practices and African folk beliefs, or the austere Protestant Dutch Church of the 17th century. In fact, they are so dissimilar it is often difficult to accept that they are of the same religion.

Throughout the history of Christianity, the ways and means of transmitting the words of Christ, the Son of God, have evolved and changed to fill the needs of disparate societies and cultures, from those of Near Eastern peasants to those of yeomen, knights, and kings of medieval Europe. The transformation of the Christian Church continues right up to the present day, where clearly differentiated regional forms of worship and understandings of the divine include many distinct evangelical sects. Among them are ones in which the precepts and ways of worship combine traditional tribal or local religions and one in which Christianity formed around indigenous conditions of governance, diet, costume, architecture, and tonsure. The mosaic of practices among the virtually countless Christian sects is a result of the divergence of understanding the texts, divine and otherwise, that guide adherents in their pursuit of a Christian life.

From its first appearance among the apostles of Jesus Christ in the 1st century CE (or AD), the number of adherents to the new religion grew exponentially. By the time of Saint Paul (c. 5–c. 65 CE), himself a remarkably effective missionary having converted from Judaism to Christianity in about 33 CE, the Christian Church had spread from Jerusalem in Palestine to Asia Minor, Greece, and Rome. In becoming a transregional religion in an inhomogeneous world, the growing number of Christian congregations combined local pagan religious traditions with their concepts of Christ, the Son of God, and with their practices in worshiping a single god. This presented problems and gave rise to questions among those who converted from polytheistic pagan beliefs to the monotheism of Christianity. In his letters to distant Christian communities, Saint Paul tried to answer the congregants' questions to bring them in line with Christ's message as Paul himself understood it.

Christianity, like its forerunner, monotheistic Judaism, began as a religion of a book. This is clear in the prologue to the Gospel, which is attributed to John the Apostle of Christ. "In the beginning was the Word, and the Word was with God, and the Word was God." Thus, *Logos*, or the Word, is a name or title of Jesus Christ. At first, this book was a collection of oral histories recounting the life of Christ. Eventually, these came to be edited, expanded, and committed to writing. For example, the Gospel of Matthew is now thought to have been composed in the late 1st century CE, and its attribution to the apostle Matthew is rejected by modern biblical scholars. Likewise, the Gospel of Mark is thought to have been written around 70 CE by an author drawing on a number of oral stories. Because the Gospels of Matthew, Mark, Luke, and John were preserved only in later copies, they were unavailable as canonical texts to the very earliest Christian churches. This led to the rise of regional variations in understanding the life and nature of Jesus Christ.

Before the Christian Church was accepted by the Roman emperor as a legitimate religion, one that was to be exempt from persecution, differences in theology and differences in worship were common, and they continued to be ubiquitous throughout the entire history of Christianity.

It is to the lively history of the church, which spans twenty-one centuries, that we can now turn.

Chapter 1 – The Apostolic Age and Pre-Nicene Christianity

The only organized religion and the only one that was trans-regional in the Roman Empire was Judaism. This monotheistic faith survived and grew slowly amidst a world dominated by paganism. The Roman version of paganism was a pan-empire, state-sanctioned, unorganized religion that was inconsistently practiced from region to region. The populace propitiated gods that were determined by local tradition. They included every form of deity, from the twelve Olympian gods of ancient Greece to lesser Greek gods, from Persian and Egyptian deities to uniquely Roman household gods. Judaism survived in this more or less chaotic world of paganism because it was generally treated as benign by Roman emperors and regional governors. It was rare for emperors to make the kind of forceful move against Jews as Titus did when he looted and then destroyed the Temple of Jerusalem in 70 CE.

In the decades following the crucifixion of Christ, his burial, and his ascension into heaven, his followers, the apostles, encouraged groups of Christians to worship together in homes and in graveyards. Christians passed on the Word of God and the message of His earthly son to families, friends, and neighbors. This first occurred in Jerusalem, where disciples gathered after establishing rudimentary Christian congregations in Galilee, as this was where Christ spent most of his life preaching. The goal was to convince Jews that the Messiah, who had long been anticipated by their prophets, whose words were preserved in what for Christians became known as the Old Testament, had indeed appeared in the human form of Jesus Christ. Jews were ripe for absorption, or rather conversion, into the new Christian faith because, at its core, Judaism was an apocalyptic religion. That is, it was focused on the eventual revelation of divine truths that were the necessary precursors to the end times. Shortly after bringing the message that the Messiah lived to the Jews, the early Christians took their message to Gentiles, or non-Jews, thus spreading Christianity beyond the place of its origins in the Holy Land.

The organization of the Christian Church can be traced back to a council held in Jerusalem in about 50 CE. At this Apostolic Council, it was decided that Gentile converts were not obliged to conform to every Jewish ritual, including the circumcision of males. However, it was decided that Jewish dietary laws were applicable to Christians. The Jewish traditions were advocated by Pharisees who had converted to Christianity. These respected Pharisees were steeped in the laws and traditions of Rabbinic Judaism, and they held that Christians must observe the Torah. The conflict between Jewish traditions and the early Christian notion that everyone should be free to accept the teachings of Jesus Christ ended with a compromise. It was agreed that for at least Gentiles, there should be few impediments placed in their path to faithfully adopting the teachings of Christ. The Council of Jerusalem became acknowledged as the foundation for all subsequent church councils.

As outsiders in Roman society, Christians naturally fell victim to hostile attacks. They were condemned for their atheism, as they did not properly acknowledge the power of the pagan gods and thus did not acknowledge the power of the emperor. In addition, the

Christians' flagrant immorality was evidenced by gossip that Christian worship services included the killing of babies and cannibalism. The latter was the stuff of conspiracy among the faithful Romans.

The persecution of Christians in the Roman Empire was not as extensive as Christian propagandists, both ancient and modern, would have us believe. Emperor Nero's henchmen and their hangers-on blamed the fiery destruction of Rome in 64 CE on Christian sedition. Christians were rounded up and subjected to torture and death. Although Christians were subjected to periodic persecution, it was not until the 3rd century that Christianity became subject to institutionalized prohibition. Emperor Decius (r. 249-251 CE) issued a decree that everyone in the empire must declare that they had sacrificed to the gods and eaten a ritual meal of sacrificial meat. This was the first formal Roman legislation with an anti-Christian intent. Those failing to meet the requirements, specifically Christians, who were adamant in their faith and unable to bribe officials, were subjected to confiscation of property, exile, torture, and possibly even death. The most violent of the formal persecutions of Christians occurred in the reign of Diocletian (r. 284-305 CE). He declared Christianity illegal and decreed that all Christian places of worship be destroyed. Christians were systematically deprived of the privileges of their rank in Roman society.

Scholars estimate that some 3,000 to 3,500 Christians were executed during the reign of Diocletian. Among those Christian martyrs were several who were subsequently canonized or recognized as saints by the Catholic Church. Saint Sebastian was one of these people. He was tied to a tree by a mob and shot with arrows. According to the story of his martyrdom, he did not succumb to his wounds. After he had recuperated, he went to Diocletian to upbraid him for his sins and was clubbed to death. Another early martyr for the faith was the virginal thirteen-year-old

Agnes, who came from a Roman noble family. She spurned a suitor who then reported her as a Christian to the authorities. Poor Agnes was dragged naked through the city of Rome, during which time all the men who had lusted after her were struck blind. She was then placed on trial and condemned to death. She was tied to the stake, and a fire was ignited at her feet. The fire, or so the story goes, miraculously passed harmlessly around her. As a last resort, a Roman officer beheaded her. Like all Christians, these martyrs could look forward to an eternal afterlife, which had been promised by Christ, who suffered a similar death at the hands of his Roman executioners.

Official Roman persecution of Christianity ended when Emperor Constantine (r. 306-337 CE) issued a proclamation known as the Edict of Milan in 313 CE, in which it was declared that Christians should be treated benevolently throughout the empire. Constantine's magnanimity toward Christians was the result of being influenced by his mother, Helena, who was a Christian, and of his belief that he had vanquished his archenemy with the aid of Christ. Constantine himself formally converted to the Christian faith and was baptized on his deathbed.

In 325 CE, Constantine, in a move to demonstrate his sympathy to the Christian Church, convened a council of Christian bishops at the city of Nicaea in present-day Turkey. The fact that the invitation went out to 1,800 bishops, as well as local and regional leaders of the Christian Church, is evidence of the rapid growth of the new religion. Modern scholars estimate that, by this time, there were as many as four million Christians in the Roman Empire. This represents an exponential growth of the faith. When Christ ascended into heaven, which, according to scripture, took place forty days after his crucifixion, sometime between 30 and 33 CE, there were only about twenty adherents of the faith. At the time of the grizzly execution of Saint Lawrence, one of the seven Christian deacons of Rome, on a gridiron in 258 CE, it is thought there were as many as three-quarters of a million Christians. (A deacon in this instance was a church official whose function, according to the Acts of the Apostles, was to provide food to widows.)

The rapid growth of the Christian faith was due in no small measure to the stories of miraculous events associated first with Christ's terrestrial life, then with the lives of his immediate apostles, and finally with the martyrs and saints who first propagated the Christian faith throughout the Roman Empire. While the largely illiterate people of the empire were unable to engage in lofty debate on theological issues, they could understand the wonder of miracles. Stories of astonishing events, such as Christ's feeding 5,000 people with bread and fishes that he miraculously multiplied for the hungry multitude and his raising Lazarus from the dead, were highly attractive to the unsophisticated. There is little doubt that the abundance of miracles in the stories of the Christian faith worked to increase the number of converts to the new religion.

The spread of Christianity to all corners of the Roman Empire presented difficulties to the unity of the Christian faith. In isolation, groups of Christians might absorb elements of local spiritual culture into their forms of worship and belief systems. These might include pagan ceremonies that were modified and adapted to Christian beliefs. For example, the Christian celebration of Christmas was an adaptation of the pagan winter solstice. It is likely that the angels prominent in the texts of the Christian faith were a modified form of flying humanoid spirits that were prominent in the cult of Mithraism, which was favored by the soldiers in the Roman army. Early Christianity has thus been characterized by several scholars as a syncretic religion amalgamating different religions, cultures, and schools of thought. Some have even proposed that the very idea of a single all-powerful God was fairly common in the Near East among pagan sects, as well as, of course, Judaism.

With such large distances separating groups of Christians by the time of Constantine, a large number of Christian groups existed who practiced their religion according to local customs. These were unsuitable to a centrally organized church. For example, in North Africa, there was a Christian sect known as the Adamites. They engaged in worship in the nude. This idea of recapturing the innocence of Adam in the garden of Eden probably came from early Christian and Jewish Gnostics (believers in personal spiritual knowledge) in the region. Other variants of Christian worship in the Apostolic Age included the Nazarenes in Palestine, who were Jewish Christians who observed the Torah as opposed to Gentile Christians who didn't. The Ebionites, also of Palestinian origin, believed that Christ was merely a man chosen by God to be His last prophet.

It was due to these vast numbers of variants in the Christian Church that Constantine called the Council of Nicaea in 325 CE. The central focus of this council was the immediate need to deal with the writings of a presbyter, Arius of Alexandria (256–336 CE). The title presbyter was derived from the organization of Jewish synagogues in which a council of ordained presbyters managed the operation and spiritual life of a faithful congregation.

Arius and his followers in Egypt believed that Jesus Christ was the Son of God and begotten by God the Father but that Christ was distinct from His father and was not co-eternal with Him. According to the Arians, Jesus Christ was born at a specific time; therefore, he was not an eternal being. His existence was thus not equivalent to that of God the Father or the Holy Ghost. For the Arians, Christ was a lesser being than God Himself. Arius's idea was rejected by the twentieth bishop of Alexandria, Athanasius (c. 296–373 CE), who believed that the Trinity—God the Father, God the Son, and the Holy Ghost—were co-equals and were all three co-eternal. The attendees at the First Council of Nicaea established the orthodox faith, coming down on the side of Athanasius. Arianism was declared a heterodox belief. In other words, it was heresy and was thus condemned by the Christian Church. This was confirmed by the Nicene Creed, a statement of Christian belief crafted by the council. This continues to be used in various forms by Christian churches to this day. It stresses that all Christians subscribe to the belief that Christ was begotten and not made by God the Father and that Christ is one being with God, or, in the words of the creed, "begotten not made, consubstantial with the father." The Nicene Creed further affirmed that Christ came down to earth and was made incarnate as a man and that he was killed but rose into heaven for the salvation of mankind. The original creed ended with the condemnation of Arian theology. It specifically says that it is incorrect to suggest that there was a time when Christ did not exist, that he was made out of nothing, that he is of another substance or essence than God Himself, or that Christ is changeable in any way.

Our knowledge of the early Christian Church's evolution depends primarily on texts, including the Acts of the Apostles and Saint Paul's letters to congregations of Christians from Galatia, a region in the south of modern-day Turkey. There are also texts by Christian theologians known as the Ante-Nicene Fathers, such as Athanasius and, before him, Origen of Alexandria (c. 184-253 CE), as well as the Carthaginian Tertullian (c. 155-c. 240 CE), and Athenagoras of Athens (c. 133-c. 190 CE). We can get a glimpse of the ideas that were the basis of the voluminous writings of the Anti-Nicene Fathers in the work of Origen. He not only translated the Hebrew text of the Bible into Greek but also interpreted many passages in it. He suggested that before creating the material universe, God created the souls of all intelligent beings. In the beginning, the souls were faithful to God, but they gradually fell into sin and were then given physical bodies. Origen wrote extensively on the relationship of the three entities of the Trinity and the incarnation of the Logos (Christ), as well as the soul, free will, and eschatology, or the ultimate destiny of humanity.

As well as theology, writers around the time of the First Nicene Council concerned themselves with the history of the Christian Church. Among them was Bishop Eusebius of Caesarea (c. 260-c. 340 CE), who wrote an *Ecclesiastical History*. It sheds considerable light on the organization and events in the history of the nascent Christian faith.

Although Eusebius was biased in his understanding of history, his work is particularly valuable in recounting the growth of Christianity through the years of persecution. When dealing with Nero's barbarism, he tells us, for example, "So it came about that this man, the first to be heralded as a conspicuous fighter against God, was led on to murder the apostles. It is recorded that in his reign Paul [in 64 CE] was beheaded in Rome itself, and that Peter likewise was crucified [between 64 and 68 CE]." Eusebius's text is rich in information on some of the heretical sects that arose in the church. For example, he informs us that Cerinthus (c.50-100 CE), according to Bishop Dionysius of Alexandria, believed "Christ's Kingdom would be on earth; and the things he lusted after himself, being the slave of his body and sensual through and through, filled the heaven of his dreams." Cerinthians were said to celebrate Christ through gluttony, lechery, sacrifices, and the immolation of victims.

Surviving material remains of the early Christian Church reveal the kind of growth suggested in written texts. The first churches were homes in which the faithful gathered. This makes perfect sense considering that the church underwent periodic suppression by Roman authorities. Secretive private worship in domestic surroundings or outside in graveyards provided the most security for the faithful. In one such house church, dating from around 232 CE and excavated in Dura-Europos, a frontier city near the Euphrates in Syria, two rooms were joined by the removal of a wall, and a dais was set up. A small room near the entrance was set up as a baptistry. These modest beginnings of Christian architecture ended when Constantine removed any official sanctions against Christianity.

Church building immediately swept the empire. In Rome, the Church of the Lateran (dedicated 324 CE) and the Church of Saint Peter (begun c. 318 CE) were built. Today, neither existing building reflects the simple yet highly functional structures of the early Christian period. Both consisted of a rectangular nave with an entrance at one end and an altar at the other, flanked by side aisles. This was the preferred plan for early churches, which was adapted from Roman basilicas or meeting halls. Along with architecture was visual art. The early Christians used the same media as their pagan contemporaries, namely, frescos, mosaics, and sculptures. They adapted pagan motifs for Christian purposes so that some art made for Christians could easily be mistaken for imperial Roman art. For example, portrait busts on sarcophagi or coffins that look like those of emperors, surrounded by decorative vines and narrative scenes under canopies and separated by columns, could be mistaken for pagan secular art were it not for the appearance of scenes with clear Christian content, such as events from the Bible like Jonah and the whale, Noah in the ark, Daniel in the lion's den, or Christ the Good Shepherd.

Chapter 2 – The Establishment and Growth of the Church in the Roman Empire

According to tradition, Christianity was brought to Rome from its birthplace in the Holy Land by Peter, one of Jesus Christ's twelve apostles. Peter, like Christ himself, was a man of low rank who worked with his hands. He was a fisherman. Christ approached Peter and his companions on Lake Gennesaret and miraculously filled their nets with fish. This, along with Christ's walking on water, which is reported in three of the gospels, and Peter's inability to do so, are the foundation stories of Peter's life as a missionary or, as Christ said, a fisher of men. The snippets of Peter's life story, as told in the four gospels of the Christian New Testament, were expanded in the Gospel of the Hebrews, known only from fragments and secondhand references in secondhand sources. Although Peter denied knowledge of Christ three times during his torture and crucifixion, it was Peter to whom Christ first appeared after he rose from the dead. Because Peter was the first to experience the truth of the Messiah's message that, through his resurrection, he would save mankind, Peter is considered the founder of the orthodox line of heirs of authority in the Christian Church. Peter's mission in propagating the message of Christ is told in the Acts of the Apostles and in Saint Paul's Epistle to the Galatians. At first, Peter led the church in Jerusalem. When he was supplanted by a faction led by the apostle James, who held to conservative views of adherence to Jewish law, Peter moved to Antioch (near the modern-day Turkish city of Antakya), where he founded a church and perhaps served as the first patriarch there. It was widely believed by later church writers that Peter went to Rome, where he became the first in the lineage of bishops of Rome, or popes, stretching to the present day.

It is uncertain exactly how much authority the Roman pope had over the Christian churches, primarily those in Asia Minor, the Holy Land, and Egypt. When Saint Paul wrote his letter to the Romans, and when he appeared in the city, he made no mention of Peter as a pope or bishop of Rome. It was probably not until Constantine's recognition of Christianity in 312 CE that the pope in Rome came to dominate the church hierarchy, exerting authority over the church in Jerusalem and the center of development of Christian theology in Alexandria. The manifestation of the primacy of Rome in church matters was implicit in the construction of the Church of Saint Peter in Constantine's time over the tomb of the martyr.

The Christian theologian, missionary, and Ante-Nicene Father Irenaeus (c. 130– c. 202 CE) wrote extensively on the history of the early Christian Church. He made a list of the popes (apostolic succession) from Saint Peter to Pope Victor I (papacy 189–199 CE). Although Irenaeus was a Greek from Smyrna, he traveled widely in the West and became a priest and then bishop of Lyon when the Christian community there was suffering under Roman persecution. Irenaeus was a third-generation Christian, and he claimed to have heard the subsequently martyred Polycarp (69–155

CE) preach. Polycarp, according to his contemporaries, was a disciple of John the Apostle.

The first detailed text revealing the beginnings of the organization of the Christian Church under the leadership of a Roman pope is a letter written by Pope Clement I (papacy 88– 89 CE) to the congregation at Corinth. The Corinthian church had undergone something of a coup with the deposition of presbyters. In his Epistle to the Corinthians, Clement said that they must reinstate the presbyters and told them that the apostles had mandated that bishops and deacons rule the church. Pope Clement said it was incumbent on all Christians that they obey their superiors. In time, the First Epistle of Clement became, along with the decisions of the Apostolic Council of around 50 CE, a foundational document for church (or canon) law.

By the time of the Council of Nicaea in 325, there were pockets of Christians throughout the Roman Empire. Substantial numbers of Christians could be found in Armenia (officially Christian c. 310 CE), Egypt, North Africa, Greece, Spain, Italy, France, central Europe, southern India (Christianized by Thomas the Apostle after 52 CE), and Ethiopia (the first bishop being appointed c. 325 CE). Syriac-speaking Christianity was centered in the Upper Mesopotamian city of Edessa, from which missionaries spread out over Mesopotamia and Persia. By 424 CE, the church leader, or first Syriac patriarch, could claim to have jurisdiction over the entire Christian Church in the eastern reaches of the Roman Empire and beyond to India and Sri Lanka.

It is argued that the swift spread of the religion was a result of its appeal to the lower classes, whose lives were significantly improved by the adoption of Christian principles. The promise of salvation, the stories of miracles, and the fact that converting one member of a household meant the conversion of an entire family have been suggested as contributors to the swift expansion of the new faith.

After the reign of Emperor Constantine and his deathbed conversion to Christianity, the church faced a single period of persecution. The crowing of Emperor Julian in 361 CE marked a short interregnum of official imperial paganism. Until his death in 363 CE, Julian, known as Julian the Apostate, instituted an empire-wide reversion to the paganism of the Hellenistic Greek world. His looking back to an earlier pre-Christian era was motivated by his desire to save the empire and restore it to its former glory. Julian's laws forbade Christians from teaching and converting unbelievers, but they were dispensed with when he died. According to rumors at the time, he was assassinated by one of his Christian soldiers. Whether this is true or not, Christians all breathed a sigh of relief when this believer of ancient myths and allegories went to his grave. The way was cleared for the expansion of the Christian religion under Valentinian the Great (r. 364-375 CE). Under Emperor Theodosius I (r. 379-395), Christianity became the official state religion of the Roman Empire. The Vestal Virgins in Rome were disbanded, and pagan rituals, all vestiges of Hellenistic religion, and the Arian heresy were outlawed. The Christian religion, as fixed at the Council of Nicaea, was made the only authorized faith.

The growth of Christianity in the immediate post-Nicaean period not only gave rise to disputes over authority, such as that claimed by the patriarch of the Persian church over the authority of the Roman church, but it also led to doctrinal disputes. The most important of these was based on the theology of Nestorius, the archbishop of Constantinople from 428 to 431 CE. As a proponent of the theological school of Antioch, he proposed that, in the union of God and Christ, the two natures, divine and human, were distinct. This ran contrary to the theology of Cyril of Alexandria (the patriarch of Alexandria from 412 to 444 CE), who, with careful political plotting, had Nestorianism condemned at the Council of Ephesus in 431. This council, convened by Emperor Theodosius II (r. 402-450 CE), was made up of about 250 bishops. It found Nestorius's concepts of the duality of Christ heretical, thus solidifying the separation of the Nestorian Persian church from that of the West.

With the increasing sophistication of the church's governance after the Councils of Nicaea and Ephesus, there arose a continuing need for a serious investigation of Christian theology through the study of the Bible, as the words and deeds of Jesus Christ and the scriptures from the Apostolic Age needed to be interpreted more fully.

Thus, early writers were foundational for the subsequent history of the church, such as the Christian scholars of the so-called Patristic era, who were known as the Great Fathers or Eight Doctors of the Church. Among those who refined Christian doctrine was Saint Ambrose, who was the bishop of Milan from 374 to 397 CE. He was a strong opponent of Arianism, about which he wrote a dense treatise. At the time, Arianism had gained widespread support among many clergy members and even Roman Emperor Valentinian II (r. 375- 392 CE). Ambrose also wrote on subjects concerning Christian ethics. He is most popularly remembered for his liberal stance on the liturgical practices of local churches, stating that "When in Rome, do as the Romans do."

Saint Jerome (c. 345-420 CE) was born in the Balkans. He studied in Rome, and then after a period of study in Trier, Germany, he moved with a group of followers into northern Syria and was ordained in Antioch. He then traveled to Constantinople and Rome. In Rome, Saint Jerome translated the New Testament from Greek into Latin. Ever restless, Jerome went to the Holy Land, visited Alexandria, and then settled down to incessant reading and writing in a cave where he produced a version of the Old Testament, commentaries on the Christian faith, and an attack on Pelagianism. This heterodox Christian concept, put forth by the theologian Pelagius (c. 355- c. 420), held that man was not born with original sin and that people were free to acquire human perfection without divine grace.

A more comprehensive refutation of Pelagianism was composed by Jerome's contemporary Saint Augustine of Hippo (354–430 CE). Baptized by Jerome in Milan in 387 CE, Augustine led a life as a noted preacher and a strong opponent of Manicheanism, a Persian religion based on the struggle between good and evil. Manicheanism was adopted by Aramaic-speaking peoples in the Near East and, at one point, was the major religious contender for dominance against Christianity. Although Augustine wrote many books and letters, it is his book, *The City of God*, that has the most enduring impact on Christian thought. In it, he dealt with such subjects as the suffering of the righteous, the existence of evil, original sin, and the conflict between free will and the omniscience of God.

The fourth Great Father, Pope Gregory (papacy 590– 604 CE), who possibly established a form of the divine liturgy, was an energetic opponent of Donatism, a heretical movement that flourished among Christians in North Africa. According to the Donatists, communion and other rites of the church could only be offered by completely pure priests.

The above four Great Fathers developed ideas for the Western branch of the church. The other four doctors of the faith helped develop foundations for the Eastern Orthodox Church. Among them were the strongly anti-Arian Athanasius of Alexandria (296–373 CE) and Basil of Caesarea (330–379), the latter of whom was the bishop of Caesarea in Asia Minor and whom wrote an influential work entitled *On the Holy Spirit*. Gregory of Nazianzus (329–390), the archbishop of Constantinople, wrote on the Trinity, which was certainly the most pressing of the ecclesiastical controversies. John Chrysostom (347–407), who later became the archbishop of Constantinople, was instrumental in the creation of a divine liturgy that was to become the Byzantine Rite as practiced in the Eastern Orthodox Church.

While the theological writings of the Great Fathers of the church, both Eastern and Western, defined and resolved matters that caused conflict within the Christian Church, there were others, often less erudite, who served as active proponents of the church's missionary function. The lives of early medieval Christian saints who took the Word of God to the nether reaches of the known earth were recorded in popular hagiographies, which praised their sanctity and their stolidness in the face of opposition by barbarians and pagans. An example of this kind of worker for the faith is Saint Patrick, who is believed to have brought Christianity to Ireland sometime in the 5th century. As the first bishop of Armagh and the primate of Ireland, Patrick promoted the conversion of Celtic polytheists. In this, he made use of miraculous powers by restoring the sight of a blind man, banishing the snakes from Ireland, turning a bowl of water into honey to cure a sick woman, driving off demons with a bell, and striking a magician dead with a bolt of lightning.

In France, an example of the Christianizing saints, those who dedicated themselves to converting pagans, is Saint Denis, who, in the 3rd century while serving as the bishop of Paris, was martyred by decapitation. This did not instantly terminate his preaching to the Franks, for the good saint, according to hagiographic literature, picked up his head and continued his sermon on repentance. This story is typical of another strain of the history of Christianity, one that is distinct from the world of sophisticated theological arguments of the Great Fathers.

The missionary work of the vast numbers of faithful adherents was enhanced by the mystery of miracles that appealed to the common folk. This aspect of Christianity, beginning with the retelling of stories of the miracles of Christ himself, was perpetuated in tales of the many Christianizing local saints, who themselves were responsible for miracles. Saint Columba (c. 521– 597) was a missionary to Ireland and the founder of the Christian Church in

Scotland. His life, or hagiography, as written by Adomnán (628-704) a century after Columba's death, includes a rich collection of stories of the saint healing people, taming wild beasts, resurrecting the dead, and stilling wild storms. The miraculous acts in hagiographies, which are ubiquitous in local folklore throughout Christendom, were instrumental in attracting the attention of potential converts and maintaining their faith after conversion. The question of the historical verification of miracles is, in large part, besides the point. What is important in understanding the effect of such supernatural events is that they were believed to be true. The same goes for stories that, for some, do not have the ring of truth. For example, it was said that the Christianization of France began with the arrival of a boatload of Christians at the mouth of the Rhone shortly after Christ's crucifixion. Among the passengers were Mary Magdalene; Mary Salome, who was believed to have witnessed the crucifixion of Christ; and another witness, Mary of Clopas. The three Marys were, according to this legend, accompanied by Joseph of Arimathea, the man who took charge of the burial of Christ. Whether this is a historical fact or not is unimportant in the chronicle of Christianity. What is significant is that these stories gained currency as an attestation of the ultimate truth of the Christian faith.

Chapter 3 – The Age of Monasticism and Scholasticism, the Rise of Universities, and the Crusades

Living a Christian life can be understood from many perspectives. Throughout history, there have been two popular ones. There are those who look outward and believe that their obligation as true believers is to convert and lead people through preaching the gospel, thus sharing the message of Christ. And there are also those who understand that to fully comprehend the divine message of Christ, it is necessary to shut oneself off from the distractions of everyday life and live an ascetic life, abstaining from all distractions of sensual pleasure. In early Christian times, those who sought the contemplative life lived as hermits in the wilderness, such as the Old Testament Prophet Elijah (c. 900 BCE- c. 849 BCE) and Saint John the Baptist (late 1st century BCE- c. 30 CE), both of whom retreated from the world for periods of reflection. Paul of Thebes (c. 226- c. 341 CE) is thought to have been the first Christian hermit completely devoted to life in isolation. He lived alone in the desert of Egypt for most of his long life. His successor in the desert was Saint Anthony of Egypt (251–356 CE), whose biography became important for the rise of Christian monasticism. It was written by Athanasius of Alexandria, and it included a story of temptation by evil demons, much like the temptation of Christ by Satan during his forty days in the Judean wilderness.

The early Christian hermits in Egypt and elsewhere in the Near East did not all live solitary lives in caves. Saint Simeon Stylites (c. 390–459 CE) chose a platform on a lofty column to spend some thirty-seven years in isolated contemplation of the divine. From his elevated home, he could communicate his visions of the Holy Spirit to the faithful flocks who gathered below. At the site of his column, which was about thirty kilometers (about nineteen miles) from Aleppo, Syria, a splendid church was erected, with construction beginning in the 5th century. It is known as *Qal at Siman*, or the "Fortress of Simeon."

Some desert-dwelling men of God chose to build huts in like-minded communities. The purpose of these communities and their internal governance were clarified by Saint Basil the Great, the bishop of Caesarea (330–379 CE). He composed a set of monastic rules that were used in the Christian Church in the East. His instructions for monastic living called for strict adherence to poverty and chastity, as well as injunctions to educate young people in schools attached to monastic communities. One of the early monastic foundations in the East was Saint Catherine's Monastery in the Sinai, which was built by Emperor Justinian I (r. 527–565 CE). It was built between 548 and 565 in honor of Saint Catherine of Alexandria (c. 287–c. 305 CE), who was martyred on orders of Emperor Maxentius (r. 306–312) on the eve of his assumption of the imperial throne. Saint Catherine was imprisoned and tortured for her faith. In prison, she was tended by angels and was fed by a dove sent down from heaven. Those who came to see her in prison were immediately converted to Christianity. When torture failed to break her faith, Catherine was placed on a spiked wheel, but when her tormentors tried to turn it and kill her, the wheel of death miraculously shattered. She was then ordered to be dispatched by beheading.

In Europe, Saint Benedict of Nursia (c. 480- c. 550 CE) composed a list of rules for those living in the twelve monastic communities he established not far from Rome. Benedict's extensive Rule, composed in 516, set out the principles for living a communal, contemplative life and how a monastery should be governed under the leadership of an abbot. Benedict acknowledged the earlier monastic rules written by Saint Basil and drew upon earlier authoritative writers in the church, such as St. Augustine. Most of Benedict's directions involved how a monk should exercise "unhesitating obedience" and be humble. Although the monks must obey their abbot, their council must be called upon in dealing with matters pertaining to the community. In a monastery, the use of speech should be moderated. There must be strict adherence to the eight canonical hours, or divisions of the day, with fixed times for prayer, which were formulated in the Apostolic Age. According to the Rule of Saint Benedict, monks were forbidden to have private possessions. The Rule of Saint Benedict regulated the work of the monks, the food they were allowed, and the books they might read. Their daily schedule of manual labor, including eating, sleeping, and prayer, was clearly defined. Abbots were instructed to offer hospitality to visitors, who were not to associate with the general population of monks. The seventy-three chapters of the Rule of Saint Benedict covered almost all aspects of monastic life. The Rule was adopted in one form or another by European Benedictine communities and was followed by other monastic orders that were founded in the Middle Ages.

After Saint Benedict, the number of monasteries in Western Christendom grew rapidly. Many were founded in Ireland, among them Clonmacnoise (544 CE). The same occurred in Scotland after the founding of a monastery at Lindisfarne in the 6th century.

Monastic establishments came to dot the European countryside. One of the largest was at Saint Gall in Switzerland, where a monastic community was founded in the first half of the 8th century over the hermitage of a solitary Irish monk named Saint Gallus (c. 550- c. 646 CE). By the early 9th century, the Abbey of Saint Gall, under the leadership of an abbot, had become a highly complex community. It boasted a series of buildings, including a large church, dormitories, kitchen, infirmary, dining hall, and farm buildings. All were constructed to serve the purposes of a self-sufficient agrarian group of contemplative monks.

The swift penetration of Europe by Benedictine monasticism was accompanied by a rise in scholarship on the Christian faith. An example of this was the work of a Benedictine monk known later as the Venerable Bede (c. 673-735 CE), who lived from time to time at Jarrow Abbey in northern England. He traveled to many abbeys in Britain, teaching and collecting information on the history of Christianity in the British Isles. Through his book, the *Ecclesiastical History of the English People*, he established himself as Britain's first historian. Aside from history and theology, Bede focused his study on the subject of *computus*, or the calculation of dates in the Christian calendar. This was an important pursuit, one in which Bede attempted to calculate the correct date for the celebration of Easter, a prime event in the Christian calendar, and to calculate the number of years since the birth of Christ, which is known as *Anno domini*, or the year of our Lord.

With the decline of the Roman Empire, the barbaric tribes, both within and beyond the imperial frontiers, slowly abandoned their nomadic lifestyles. At about the same time, they were subject to conversion to Christianity by the likes of the 5th-century Saint Patrick in Ireland. King Clovis I, who succeeded in unifying the Frankish tribes under his authority, was baptized a Christian by Saint Remigius (437- 533 CE), the bishop of Reims, in 496. The East Germanic tribes in what is today the Ukraine and Romania were converted to the Christian faith in the late 4th century by Ulfilas (c. 311- 383), who also translated the Bible into the Gothic language.

The Christian secular leaders in Europe in the early stages of the rise of monarchies and princedoms obtained their temporal authority by means of force. Beginning in the 5th century, the Roman leaders of the Christian Church, the popes, also exerted temporal power, acquiring control over land in the Italian Peninsula that became known as the Papal States. From these estates, the popes drew on the nobles for service, who provided military support from time to time. A certain portion of agricultural produce was also rendered to the papal court. The fact that temporal power was claimed by the papacy led to conflicts with secular kings and princes throughout the Middle Ages. One of the documents that the popes used to support their claim to secular, political authority over kings and potentates was the *Donation of Constantine*. It was purportedly a decree from Emperor Constantine that granted the pope political authority over the western parts of the Roman Empire. The document was exposed as a forgery by a Renaissance humanist scholar in the 15th century. Today, it is thought that the *Donation of Constantine* was penned sometime in the 8th century.

Charlemagne (r. 800–814 CE) rose to dominance as the king of the Franks in 768. In 800, he journeyed to Rome, where he was crowned as the Holy Roman emperor by the pope, thus receiving divine recognition for his position as the greatest ruler in Europe since the era of the Romans and confirming his position as a secular leader subservient to the pope. Whether Charlemagne's secular power was conferred on him by the pope acting as God's regent on Earth or whether he obtained this power strictly through secular means was not clear in the coronation ceremony. The question remained for the history of Europe, up until the modern era, whether the Christian God worked solely through the authority of His vice-regent on Earth, the pope, or whether He selected specific sovereigns to be His vice-regents on Earth. Throughout the history of the church in the Middle Ages, the conflict between the pope and secular leaders was framed around the rights of the latter to unilaterally exact taxes on ecclesiastical institutions, such as monasteries, and to appoint church authorities.

The pope himself was not the only man of the church who depended on a system of rents and allegiances that became known as the feudal system. As they expanded, many monastic communities required more and more agricultural land for the monks' sustenance. They also depended on the surrounding nobles for protection. Monasteries under the leadership of abbots thus became integral parts of European feudalism. Rents in the form of agricultural produce and labor on monastic lands, as well as military service owed by subservient nobles, had the effect of raising some monastic establishments to a very high level in the councils of superior kings and princes. For example, princely or imperial abbeys in the Holy Roman Empire came to have a special immediacy to the imperial throne. Prince-abbots came to be advisors to the emperor, and as such, they occupied positions that created a dual-allegiance to their secular leader and the pope.

The predominance of secular power claimed by sovereigns over certain Christian communities meant that there was continual friction between the papacy and independence-minded leaders of states. This often led to war. The problem was exacerbated when secular nobles founded or financed monastic establishments. By the 10th century, most European monasteries were privately owned, and the secular proprietors claimed the authority to appoint abbots and officials. In many cases, these posts were filled by unqualified churchmen, and the behavior of their monks became lax.

In an effort to reform monastic life, which still nominally followed the Rule of Saint Benedict, William I, Duke of Aquitaine (875-918 CE), founded a monastery at Cluny in 910. The monks were to follow the purest lives of contemplative worship, foster the use of fine art in rendering praise to God, and care for the poor. To prevent the monastery from sliding into secular abuses, Duke William made the governance of the Abbey of Cluny entirely subservient to the papacy. Without secular interference, the Cluniac or Reformed Benedictines grew in number, and several abbeys were founded in France, England, Italy, and Spain. This notion that the Cluniac Benedictines were entirely under the control of the papacy was breached over and over again by secular potentates who resented the control of large parts of their economies by the papacy.

A monk from Cluny named Robert de Molesme (1028-1111) found that even the reformed Cluniac monasteries were tainted with lax behavior. He obtained permission to establish a monastery where strict and severe Benedictine principles were practiced. He and a group of followers founded a monastery at Cîteaux near Dijon in France in 1098. Perhaps because of the austere order's strict organization, the monastery did not immediately attract enough monks to ensure its viability. In 1112, a Burgundian nobleman named Bernard (1090-1153 CE) and around thirty of his friends joined the Abbey at Cîteaux, thus setting the stage for the growth of the Order of the Cistercians. Bernard was charged by the abbot of Cîteaux to establish a Cistercian abbey at Clairvaux, where the reputation of Bernard's holiness and, no doubt, his connections to the nobility resulted in such rapid expansion of his abbey that it, in turn, founded new monasteries in various dioceses throughout what is now France.

The most important building in a medieval monastic community was the church. These often massive structures were built in the Romanesque style—a combination of ancient Roman architectural motifs such as pilasters, columns, barrel vaults, and semi-circular arches, as well as Eastern Christian Church motifs, a basilican plan, and domical and semi-dome roofs. The Romanesque abbey churches, such as those in France at the Benedictine abbey at Vézelay (1120-1150), Saint-Sernin at Toulouse (c. 1118), and the contemporary Abbey Church of Sainte-Foy in Conques were constructed not just for monkish worshippers but were also decorated with sculptures and wall paintings illustrating Old and New Testament stories, which served as a kind of visual Bible for the faithful illiterate peasants as well as for the wealthier pilgrims who passed through town on their way through France. Oftentimes, they would be heading over the Pyrenees into Spain to visit Santiago da Compostela, where the relics of Saint James were housed. To encourage pilgrims to stop at specific monasteries, take advantage of the hospitality, and make substantial gifts, monasteries along the pilgrimage roads vied to offer efficacious relics. For example, the monks of Conques offered the relics of the 4th-century Christian martyr Sainte-Foy. At Toulouse, pilgrims could approach the relics of Saint Saturnin (died 257 CE), one of the first seventy-two disciples of Christ in France. He was dragged around Toulouse by a bull after refusing to honor the Roman pagan gods. Vézelay Abbey housed the relics of Mary Magdalene, which undoubtedly were attractive to pious pilgrims. These relics were so important to the income of monasteries that it was not unknown for the monks of one institution to raid another and make off with significant saintly relics.

In the Eastern Greek-speaking half of the Roman Empire, the Christian Church developed along different lines from the Latin-speaking West. Constantine's foundation of his "new Rome," Constantinople (modern-day Istanbul), settled over the ancient town of Byzantium, set the stage for the divergence of the Christian Church. With the exception of his nephew, Emperor Julian the Apostate (r. 361–363 CE), who rejected Christianity and fostered a revival of Hellenistic Greek culture, the so-called Byzantine emperors at Constantinople managed the church from their courts, as did the pope in Rome. Of particular importance in the evolution of the Eastern Christian Church was the long-lasting debate over whether religious images, particularly those of Christ, were acceptable as adjuncts to worship. Some Byzantine emperors, such as Leo III (r. 717–741 CE), persuaded by court theological scholars, declared that the veneration of images was idolatry. Eventually, proponents of visual representations of the divine succeeded in overcoming the iconoclasts. As a result, the decoration of churches in the East came to equal that in the West. The controversy over images in the church persisted up to and beyond the early years of Protestantism in Europe.

The churches in the Byzantine Empire were different in physical form from those in the West. They were distinguished by domes supported by heavy lofty walls and equally substantial round-headed arches. The large interior spaces were decorated with mosaics. Within these structures, worship was carried out according to forms determined by the time of year and the Christian feasts. These liturgies, or Eucharistic services of what became known as the Byzantine Rite, were developed in the East from the writings of John Chrysostom and Saint Basil the Great (previously mentioned as the Great Fathers of the Eastern Orthodox Church), both of whose liturgies find their origins in early Christian adaptations of Jewish liturgy.

Under the auspices of the Byzantine emperor, church councils were held in the East after that at Nicaea in 325. These councils intended to deal with heterodoxy beliefs within the church. For instance, the Second Council of Constantinople of 553 attempted to stamp out Nestorian theology, which, as we have seen, resulted in the separation of the Persian Nestorian church from that practiced in Byzantium and Europe. The pope in Rome objected to some of the findings of the council. This led to a temporary separation, or schism, between some of the churches in northern Italy that were dependent on the patriarch of Constantinople and the papacy in Rome.

The principal expansion of the Eastern Church was a result of the work of two saints: the brothers Cyril (c. 826- 869) and Methodius (815–885). According to historical documents, Cyril conducted his first missionary expedition among the Khazars in

860. After returning to Constantinople, Cyril and Methodius set out to bring Christianity as practiced by the Byzantine Church to Moravia (part of the modern-day Czech Republic). To facilitate their work, they invented a script known as Cyrillic, one of the oldest known Slavic alphabets, to aid in their translations of the gospels and liturgical texts in Slavic. In Moravia, missionaries were sent out by the Frankish Carolingian court. These churchmen were proponents of the Latin liturgy. To avoid a conflict with the Moravian authority, which the archbishop of Salzburg believed to belong to him, Pope Nicholas I (papacy 858–867 CE) summoned Cyril and Methodius to Rome. They were permitted to continue to use their Slavic alphabet. The decision was subsequently overridden, and after the death of Cyril, Methodius was briefly imprisoned by European bishops who accused him of heterodox behavior.

The work of Saints Cyril and Methodius, in particular, the translation of Christian texts into Slavic, was instrumental in the Christianization of Kievan Rus'. According to the annals of the history of Kievan Rus', as recorded in the *Primary Chronicle* or *Chronicle of Nestor*, dating from around 1113, the first Christian ruler of Kievan Rus' was Vladimir the Great (r. 980–1015 CE). He turned a large swath of the region north of the Black Sea into a Christian kingdom that owed allegiance to the church in Constantinople.

The expansion of the influence of the Eastern Orthodox Church in Constantinople exacerbated a long-brewing dispute between the Eastern and Western churches. Among the unresolved issues was the relationship between the Holy Ghost and God the Father and His Son, Jesus Christ. The two branches of the Christian Church could also not agree on whether leavened or unleavened bread should be used in the celebration of the Eucharist. On top of these theological differences, the bishop of Rome (the pope) claimed universal jurisdiction, thus confirming the inferiority of the authority of the archbishop or patriarch of Constantinople. The dispute came to a head when the pope demanded that the churches in southern Italy conform to the practices of the Latin Church or be closed. In retaliation, the patriarch of Constantinople ordered the closure of all churches using the Latin liturgy in Constantinople. This, in turn, led to a formal schism in 1054 between the Greek Church in the East and the Latin Church in the West.

Along with the expansion of the Eastern Orthodox Church, there was a rising movement of piety in Europe, which was led by Saint Bernard of Clairvaux. His new monastic establishment became swamped with new monks. To manage the overflow, new monasteries were founded in France. Bernard himself wrote extensively on the rules of the Order of the Cistercians, encouraging disciplined contemplative spirituality in isolated communities.

The Christian Church in the East, particularly in the Holy Land, came under siege by Islamic Turks. Adherents to the new monotheistic religion of Islam, which was founded by the Prophet Muhammad (571-632 CE), were harassing Christian pilgrims in the Holy Land. The emperor of Byzantium, Alexios I Komnenos (r. c. 1081-1118), asked the pope for military assistance in freeing the Holy Land from the scourge of Muslims. Pope Urban II (papacy 1088-1099) responded favorably, in part motivated by the potential of reuniting the Eastern and Western churches under his own authority. Urban urged the kings, princes, and knights of Europe to take up the cross and join a crusade to free the Holy Land from the scourge of "infidels" or unbelievers. The First Crusade (1096-1099) before getting underway is marked by the first European massacre of Jews. The deadly riot of Crusaders, who were itching to fight, took place in Germany while troops were mustering for their journey to the East. Up until this time, unconverted Jews were more or less regarded with benign neglect by European Christians. The pre-Crusade outburst of anti-Semitism by Christian soldiers marked the beginnings of centuries of institutionalized Christian Church prejudice against Jews in Europe.

The warriors in the First Crusade were successful in dislodging the Islamic Turks from Jerusalem, after which they established the Latin Kingdom of Jerusalem under the leadership of a French prince. With Christian control came the proliferation of the Christian Church in the Near East and the confirmation of an ecclesiastical hierarchy that owed allegiance to the Latin Church in Rome. This incursion of Latin Christianity into territories formerly under the auspices of the patriarch of Constantinople led to conflict, which was expressed in minor battles between Byzantine Christians and Western Christians.

In the Near East, the Kingdom of Jerusalem, founded in 1099, was subject to internecine struggles over the succession to the crown and incursions of Turks from Persia. A greater danger to the Kingdom of Jerusalem was the rise in power of regional Islamic sects. With the establishment of Christian authority over Jerusalem and the surrounding lands of the Holy Land, the numbers of Christian pilgrims to the Near East grew. The journey from the Mediterranean port of Jaffa to the sites of Christ's life on Earth was fraught with danger for pilgrims. They were periodically attacked by Islamic warriors and highwaymen, so a monastic order was founded to protect these pilgrims. The Templar Order was stationed on the Temple Mount in Jerusalem. Over time, the order came to be financed by donations solicited by Saint Bernard of Clairvaux. It quickly grew to become the richest monastic order, with houses not only in the Holy Land but also throughout Europe. In 1139, Pope Innocent II (papacy 1130–1143) exempted the Templar Order from local taxes, allowing it to become even more wealthy and an even more serious threat to secular leaders whose income depended on the taxation of ecclesiastical establishments.

The Persians took Edessa in Upper Mesopotamia in 1144. Thus, the Second Crusade was called by Pope Eugene III (papacy 1145-1153), who enlisted the help of Bernard of Clairvaux, the most influential churchman in the West, to preach the cause. At the city of Vézelay, France, Bernard addressed a crowd of the faithful, which included King Louis VII of France (r. 1137-1180). The king and a great number of the French nobility took up the cross, as did the common people. Bernard then went to Germany, where he succeeded in convincing Conrad III, King of the Holy Roman Empire (r. 1138-1152), and his nobles to take up the cross. Before leaving Europe, the German Crusaders perpetrated another massacre of Jews. On their arrival in the Holy Land in 1148, the Crusaders suffered a major defeat at the hands of the Muslims. When they finally departed the Levant in 1150, they left such a severely weakened Kingdom of Jerusalem that, in 1187, the city itself fell to Islamic forces. This loss precipitated the launching of the Third Crusade in 1189, which was led by Western Christendom's most powerful secular leaders, the kings of France and England and the Holy Roman emperor. The Third Crusade was partially successful in restoring much of the Holy Land to Christian control, but it failed to dislodge the Muslims from Jerusalem. From this point on, subsequent crusades, which include the Fourth (1202-1204), the Fifth (1217-1221), the Sixth (1228-1229), the Seventh (1248-1254), failed to establish Christian dominance in the Near East.

In Europe, during the period of the Crusades, the church was in a constant struggle to maintain the pope's authority and to ensure that the faith remained free from heterodox ideas. Heretical Christianity, such as in the form practiced by the Cathars in southern France and the Waldensians, was a constant thorn in the side of the church establishment. The Cathars were primarily a French sect that believed in the principle of two gods. The good god of the New Testament was countered by the evil god of the Old Testament. This dualistic approach was anathema to the Catholic

Church, which held the orthodox view that there was only one God, the creator of all things. The Cathars' religion was centered in the French town of Albi. Thus, they were known as Albigensians. After being condemned as heretics by church councils, the Cathars were effectively forced into hiding by the victorious knights and soldiers of the genocidal Albigensian Crusade in 1229. The same occurred with the Waldensians, a proto-Protestant movement that began in Lyon, France, in the late 12th century. Following the leadership of Peter Waldo (c. 1140-c. 1205), the Waldensians believed in obtaining Christian spiritual purity through poverty and strict adherence to the Christian precepts as stated in the Bible. The Waldensians were declared heretics in 1215, and they were persecuted and nearly annihilated before undergoing a revival in the Protestant Reformation in the 17th century.

In order to ensure that the heretical culprits such as the Cathars were identified and forced to recant their beliefs, an inquisition system was developed by the church. In 1252, the pope authorized the use of torture by inquisitors in dealing with heretics through a papal bull. Later, the newly formed orders of Dominican and Franciscan friars were assigned the role of managing court procedures for handling heretical Christians. The inquisition reached the apex of its activity in Spain in the 15th century. Throughout the Spanish dominions, inquisition courts were busy forcing conversions of Muslims and Jews to the Christian faith. The most feared of these inquisitors was Tomás de Torquemada (1420–1498), a Dominican friar who became the first grand inquisitor in Spain. His name has become synonymous with the cruelty, religious intolerance, and fanaticism of the Spanish Inquisition.

The Crusades can be seen as a combination of Christian obligation by the nobility and the common people of Europe to combat non-believers under the banner of the cross and a continent-wide desire to exert secular dominance through force. One of the results of the Crusades in the Christian kingdoms of

Europe was a rise in piety and the spread of Christ's message. As a result of this, a number of new orders of Christian monks were founded. They often followed in the footsteps of Bernard Clairvaux and his expansion of the Order of the Cistercians.

For example, St. Francis of Assisi founded the Franciscan Order in 1209. His rules for his followers called for them to live an austere life, following that of Jesus Christ. From their humble monasteries, they went out into their communities to preach the Word of God to the common people, first in Italy and then throughout Christian Europe. A second order was soon founded by the Franciscans in 1212, called the Order of Saint Clare. This was a contemplative cloistered order of nuns, and it, too, spread quickly throughout Europe.

Saint Dominic (1170-1221), a Spanish monk, founded an order of mendicant, or poor, preaching friars in 1216. The Dominicans considered themselves to be purer in their lifestyle than contemporary orders who had, over the years, become wealthy landowners and major participants in the wielding of power in the secular world.

While these orders expanded the missionary work of the church, refinements in Christian theology were being made in newly formed universities. Education, which was necessary for the advancement of the Christian faith, was first offered in schools attached to cathedrals or major monastic foundations. With the rise of monasticism in Europe, schools were established to educate the sons of local nobles. One of the most highly reputed schools arose at the Chartres Cathedral in France. In the 11th and 12th centuries, this school attracted an illustrious array of scholars who contributed theological treatises, or studies of natural philosophy, to what is known as the 12th-century renaissance. This period was marked by the rise of scholasticism. It employed dialectical reasoning to resolve apparent theological contradictions. This form of inquiry was adopted at universities, which gradually came to supplant monastic and cathedral schools as centers for liberal arts education. The curriculum was divided into the quadrivium—arithmetic, geometry, music, and astronomy—and the trivium—grammar, logic, and rhetoric. The purpose of this education system was to enable the propagation of the Word of God and to eventually serve the needs of individuals employed in secular and ecclesiastical bureaucracies.

The foundation of universities at Bologna, Paris, and Oxford in the 12th century, as well as Palencia and Salamanca in Spain, Padua and Naples in Italy, and Toulouse and Orléans in France in the first half of the 13th century, are evidence of the sudden emergence of the demand for education and the rise in Christian scholarship during the period of the Crusades. The church was the beneficiary of many scholastic teachers and thinkers who wrote extensively on theological matters, exploring the thorny issues of Christianity. Among the best known today is Saint Thomas Aquinas (1225-1274), a Dominican friar who studied at the University of Paris. He became a teacher in Cologne, Paris, and Rome. Saint Thomas was a colleague of a fellow Dominican scholar named Albertus Magnus (c. 1200-1280). Albertus's output in scholastic writings, while considerably less than Aquinas, nevertheless exemplifies the breadth of scholarship at the time. He wrote on astronomy, music, morals, and theories of justice and natural law. However, some of the writings of the scholastics did not sit well with orthodox church theology. William of Ockham (1285-1347), a Franciscan friar, had his works condemned as unorthodox by a synod of bishops. He was ordered to appear before the papal court at Avignon in 1324, where he defended his notion that Jesus and the apostles owned no property and that the Franciscans were correct in following a rule that forbade individual or communal ownership of property. After fleeing Avignon, William of Ockham was excommunicated, after which he wrote that Pope John XXII (papacy 1316-1334) was himself a heretic for opposing the doctrine of apostolic poverty and hence the Rule of Saint Francis.

Although the scholars of monastic schools and the new universities wrote extensively on theological subjects using the scholastic method, there were other means for the communication of truths of the Christian faith. In the Middle Ages, the common folk, those who toiled in the fields and served the small towns of farmers and their families, did not partake in the great events happening in the Christian Church. They were illiterate and led short lives of what we today would consider miserable. The peasants only went on Crusades as servants to their overlords or served as foot soldiers, spear carriers, and archers. Those who went as a part of a noble's train were a part of the excess population not required to work the land at home. They were not particularly driven by faith in the Christian cause. However, they did believe the myths and legends of the faith. These were conveyed to them in the simplest of stories by priests and preaching friars. Of course, they were not always written down in manuscripts as they were of lesser importance to the church than the Bible and the scholarly commentaries on it. Some of the stories consumed by the peasantry were compiled in the 13th century. Jacobus de Varagine (c. 1230-c. 1299), the Dominican archbishop of Genoa, told of saints' lives, including the fabulous tales of miracles, in his *Legenda Aurea* (the *Golden Legend*). These were the kind of tales that inspired the illiterate to adhere to Christian doctrines of morality. Jacobus's work was quickly translated into the vernacular languages of Europe so that it could be consulted by preachers seeking material that would appeal to their peasant flocks. It should also be noted that outside of major monasteries and cathedral towns, ecclesiastics in the Christian Church were often marginally literate and unschooled in the finer points of theology. Being outside the purview of ecclesiastical authorities, they were apt to fall into heretical practices and tell stories that were more derived from secular folktales than from canonical scriptures. This only began to change in the 15th century when towns became magnets for the population, allowing greater numbers of the faithful to have access to more sophisticated services of worship.

Because of the vast reach of the Christian Church, there were constant rumblings in various archiepiscopal regions, namely in France, England, and the Holy Roman Empire in regards to the Latin Church, and in Russia, Asia Minor, and the Balkans in regards to the Eastern Church. Some of these involved disputes over theology, but more often, it was over who should control the church in feudal societies, with a king or other nobleman as the secular leader. The most profound of these political differences was in France, whose leader, King Philip IV (r. 1285-1314), aggressively attacked the pope in Rome. His target was Pope Boniface VIII (papacy 1294-1303), who was responsible for reorganizing canon or church law. King Philip's imposition of taxes on the clergy in his kingdom and their ban from taking part in his administration was condemned by Boniface, who claimed these powers over the clergy. After Philip publicly burnt a copy of Boniface's encyclical, or bull, claiming supreme authority, the pope excommunicated the French king. French forces were sent to capture the pope in Italy. During his three days imprisoned by the French, Boniface was beaten so badly that he died shortly after his release. Philip IV then forced the cardinals, who were the electors of the pope, to appoint a Frenchman named Clement V (papacy 1305-1314) as the pontiff. Clement set up his papal court in Avignon, which was then part of the Holy Roman Empire, abutting Philip IV's Kingdom of France to the north. The establishment of the papal court outside Rome became known as the Avignon Papacy, as well as the Babylonian Captivity, as people drew comparisons of the papacy to the captivity of the ancient Jews in Babylon. The Avignon Papacy lasted through the reign of seven French popes. In 1377, Pope Gregory XI (papacy 1370-1378) moved his court back to Rome.

While scholasticism continued to thrive in European universities in the 14th century, a divergent mode of understanding the meaning of the Christian texts and Christ's life arose. This was a more immediate form of spiritual communication with the divine that did not require extensive reading of ancient texts and sophisticated treatises on theology. During the Avignon Papacy, the church was in some disarray, as secular leaders and the papacy clashed over authority, and the Franciscan and Dominican orders vied for papal favor. A Dominican, Eckhart von Hochheim (c. 1260-c. 1328), known as Meister Eckhart, preached in vernacular German on the presence of God in the individual soul and on suffering and detachment. The mystical approach of Eckhart was carried on by a group of spiritual heirs called the Friends of God. These Dominicans and laypersons practiced direct communication with the divine through prayer and contemplation.

The strain of mystical piety in Europe was furthered by Brigit of Sweden (c. 1303-1373). Beginning in her youth, she had visions of the Passion of Christ. These profoundly affected her belief in the immediacy of the divine. She lived a life of extreme poverty and dedicated herself to the needs of the poor. To broaden the impact of her mystical union with God, she founded the Order of the Most Holy Savior, known as the Bridgettines, for nuns and monks.

The devastation wreaked by the Black Death between 1346 and 1353, which killed perhaps as many as a quarter of the population of Europe, had a profound effect on the Christian Church. Some thought that the horrendous plague presaged the second coming of the Messiah. Groups of flagellants took to the streets of towns and cities, where they publicly scourged themselves with whips. By doing this, the common folk emulated the torture of Christ in the hopes that through self-mortification, they could achieve forgiveness for their sins and be quickly carried up to heaven should they succumb to the plague. For the pope, the notion that flagellants could, in a sense, absolve their own sins was heretical, as this was the sole prerogative of ordained priests. In 1372, Pope Gregory XI (papacy 1370-1378) ordered his ecclesiastical court of inquisitors to stamp out the flagellant movement. The Black Death, which was still feared well after it was over, inspired an English woman who was stricken with illness and had visions on her supposed deathbed of the Passion of Christ. These mystical connections to the divine were recorded by Julian of Norwich (1343-1416) in what was to be the first book written by an English woman, *Revelations of Divine Love*. While Julian's influence on the development of the Christian Church was limited in the Middle Ages, that of the mystic Catherine of Siena (1347-1380) in Italy was broader. At the age of twenty-one, Catherine experienced a mystical marriage with Christ. She traveled about northern Italy, preaching the message of reforming the clergy. She also told the common folk that they could repent by submerging themselves in total love of God. At Pisa, Catherine preached for obedience to the pope and promoted the launching of a new crusade. It was there, while in a mystical trance, that she received the stigmata (the wounds of Christ at the crucifixion), which only she herself could see. Catherine also involved herself in church affairs by supporting the movement of the papal court from Avignon back to Rome.

The rise of mystical forms of Christianity in the Late Middle Ages is a phenomenon that has intrigued scholars in the modern world, as today, feminist theology has begun to have an impact. One explanation of the female mystics' visions is that they were holy anorexics. Whether their form of communication with Christ and God was brought on by neurological conditions or not, it is clear that mystical Christianity reached an unprecedented level in the years around the Black Death.

When called upon to elect a new pope in 1378, the College of Cardinals elected Pope Urban VI, who received the support of Catherine of Siena. However, because of the quarrelsome nature of Urban, the cardinals annulled their choice and elected Robert of

Geneva as Pope Clement VII (papacy 1378-1394). Clement went to Avignon, where he and his successors reigned as anti-popes until the end of the Papal Schism at the Council of Constance (1414-1418).

The Council of Constance, called by Sigismund, King of the Romans and Hungary (Holy Roman Emperor 1433-1437), was attended by about thirty cardinals and a large number of ecclesiastical scholars of the law, abbots, and bishops. The first order of business was to solve the problem of the three contending popes and install a single new pope, Martin V (papacy 1417-1431). The second challenge to the authority of the church to be dealt with at Constance were heretical movements in the church inspired by the Czech theologian Jan Hus (c. 1372-1415) and the English theologian and teacher at Oxford University John Wycliffe (c. 1320-1384). Hus had argued that the church had fallen into error, if not outright corruption, in selling indulgences (advance remission of punishment in purgatory for sins). Hus was excommunicated and summoned to Constance, where he was summarily imprisoned. After refusing to recant his position, Hus was burned at the stake. The followers of Hus, called Hussites, in Bohemia and Moravia refused to bow to the authority of the church.

The situation with John Wycliffe's heresy in England was even more difficult for the church. He had the Bible translated into vernacular English so that its message could be understood by the common folk. Wycliffe and his followers, who were called Lollards, questioned several of the tenets of the orthodox faith. Among them were objections that particularly fell afoul of the church. These included the Lollards' unorthodox beliefs on the separation of secular and religious power, predestination, the veneration of saints, and the very legitimacy of the institution of the papacy. Wycliffe was first condemned for the notion that the church had fallen into the sin of luxury and that it should divest itself of all its property. Wycliffe believed that the clergy should live a life of poverty. Pope

Gregory XI (papacy 1370–1378) had published a bull condemning Wycliffe's ideas. As a preemptory move, Wycliffe published a text in which he argued that the excommunicated could appeal the charge to the king and royal court. Wycliffe escaped being branded as a heretic and spent the twilight years of his life writing a text rejecting transubstantiation, the belief that the bread and wine of the Eucharist were transformed into the body and blood of Christ. Wycliffe was punished post-mortem at the Council of Constance, where his writings were banned. Wycliffe was also *de facto* excommunicated retroactively.

From the mid-12th century onward, the physical manifestation of the Christian Church became more and more elaborate. Monastic churches, cathedrals, and parish churches became progressively lighter and more suffused with light, and at the same time, there was a desire among church builders to make their structures ever taller. This was the Gothic style, characterized by pointed arches, thinner walls, and large windows with stained glass. Beginning in the mid-12th century, first in France and then elsewhere in Europe, builders and masons developed refined means of engineering that allowed for progressively more impressive ecclesiastical structures. Around their churches, towns arose. Even today, the church is the central feature of the urban fabric.

Prior to the rise of cities, the wealth of Europe was concentrated in the church. While the nobility occupied impressive structures, such as manor houses and castles, for the most part, they were not ostentatious in their patronage of artists working on domestic surroundings. Most of the surviving art of the Middle Ages was intended for use in the church or was created to confirm a nobleman's relationship to the church. In the visual arts, such as sculptures, wall paintings, manuscript illuminations, and eventually altar paintings on wood, the heavy and often unrealistic forms of humans of the Romanesque period were supplanted by more and more realistic and graceful figures, as well as naturalistic animals and vegetation. Christian artists and architects looked outward into the world for inspiration and reflections of the divine in nature.

Chapter 4 – The Reformation and the Counter-Reformation

In the 16th century, the Latin Church under the auspices of the pope in Rome was subjected to criticism for its claims to secular authority, abuses among the clergy, theological discrepancies, and errors in understanding the Holy Scriptures. This was in part due to the increasing number of literate people among the secular population and the increasing wealth and commerce conducted in urban centers. Gradually, Europe became less and less an agrarian society where people lived in isolation and more and more a society of urban merchants and tradesmen. There was no equivalent of this in the East, where the influence of the Christian Church continued to expand with few interruptions caused by dissident Christians.

The proto-Protestant movements begun by John Hus in Bohemia and Moravia and John Wycliffe in England are but two examples of dissenting groups that arose in Europe in the Late Middle Ages. Fundamental to the upsurge in church reform movements across the continent was the increasing ability of access to the Bible. The word of the Christian faith, which was previously available to only those who could afford handmade manuscript copies, suddenly became widely dispersed through printed Bibles that were first published by Johannes Gutenberg (c. 1400-1468) in 1455. The text was soon translated into the languages of various national groups in Europe. The first printed translation of the Bible in vernacular French was published by a press in Antwerp in 1530. A complete Bible in German was published in 1534, which included a New Testament in German translated by Martin Luther (1483-1546) that had been published in 1522. In England, William Tyndale (c. 1494-1536) and others produced a new translation of the Bible in 1535 using Greek and Hebrew texts, Luther's New Testament, and a new Latin edition of the New Testament by Desiderius Erasmus (1469-1536). Erasmus was a Dutch scholastic priest who, through his writings, would become a giant of Renaissance humanism. The rise of humanism had a revolutionary impact on the theology of the Christian Church. It stressed the value of human beings, the freedom of mankind, and progress in society. In essence, the humanistic approach to theology and philosophy diminished the unquestioning power of the divine to order every aspect of human life.

Martin Luther, a priest with experience in living a monastic life, became a professor of theology at the University of Wittenberg in Germany. When a Dominican monk was charged with selling indulgences to finance the rebuilding of Saint Peter's in Rome, Luther was driven to action, stating his opinions on the sale of indulgences and the wealth of the Latin Church. His arguments in the form of Ninety-five Theses were, it was said, publicly displayed by being nailed to the door of a church in Wittenberg on October 31st, 1517. These statements on the church regarding its organization and various aspects of theology immediately caught the attention of local ecclesiastics. More dangerous for the church was the publication of these heretical comments and their distribution throughout Germany and abroad. Pope Leo X (papacy 1513-1521) sent emissaries to examine Martin Luther and to convince him to bring his thinking in line with the orthodox faith. This failed, and Luther was excommunicated in 1521 for his questioning of the papal authority. In the same year, Luther was taken before a secular court, the Diet (or Parliament) of Worms, where he refused to recant his writings. Following the meeting of the Diet, the Holy Roman emperor had an edict published that outlawed Luther and banned his writings. Luther was imprisoned shortly after. While incarcerated, he continued to write texts, objecting to the church's notions of the Eucharist, confession, and monastic vows, as well as other topics. Some of his more radical followers, known as the Zwickau prophets, instigated an insurrection. This was a revolt of the peasantry against the upper class based on the heretical notion that there was equality among men and that Christ's return to Earth was imminent. After Martin Luther was released from prison, he preached and wrote vehemently against the German Peasants' War, saying that the insurgents should accept secular authority and that their violence was the work of the devil, although he concurred with some of their grievances. With the defeat of the peasants in 1525, Luther set about establishing a new church under temporal authority. He wrote a German Mass, published in 1526, which was intended to satisfy the common people by giving them access to what was obscure to them in the Latin Mass. Although the Eucharist remained the focus of Luther's liturgy, he allowed for the divestment of the clergy and the absence of other symbols of ecclesiastical authority and added the singing of hymns by the congregants in German and communal recitation of the Nicene Creed to the service. At a meeting of the Diet of the Holy Roman Empire at Speyer in 1529, followers of Luther protested against the Catholic authorities who were present, fearing that if the churchmen prevailed, it would mean the end of any future reform of the church. Hence, the movement for the new church became known as Protestantism.

Luther's reforms were insufficient for Swiss theologian Huldrych Zwingli (1484–1531). He created a new communion liturgy and railed against the use of images in churches, which, over the years, had accumulated veritable museums of religious art. Although he met with Martin Luther, the two could not resolve their differences. This meant that a unified reformed church could not be formed. Among the followers of Zwingli's reforms was a group of radicals who objected to Zwingli's subservience to the secular Council of Zurich, with particular reference to the baptism of infants. The ideas of the Anabaptists flourished and spread to neighboring cantons in Switzerland and then abroad into Germany and the Low Countries, where their cause was taken up by the Catholic priest Menno Simons (1496-1561). Menno formally rejected the Catholic Church and the priesthood in 1536. His followers, who called themselves Mennonites, soon came to be a force to be reckoned with in the Protestant Reformation. Earlier, a French preacher, John Calvin (1509-1564), had broken with the Catholic Church and fled persecution for his ideas on predestination (the idea that all events in this world have been willed by God) and the absolute sovereignty of God working through the Holy Ghost in the salvation of man. He settled temporarily in Switzerland.

Calvin's theology was, in part, adopted by another reformed congregation in Geneva. These exiles from England were religious refugees who fled persecution under the Roman Catholic Queen Mary I (r. 1553-1558). These Protestants were committed to the breakaway Christian Church founded in England by Henry VIII (r. 1509-1547). Henry had established what became known as the Church of England in opposition to papal authority. The dispute that precipitated this schism was the pope's refusal to annul one of Henry VIII's marriages. Henry's assumption of leadership of the Christian Church in England involved his expulsion of all those ecclesiastics who swore allegiance to the pope, the dissolution of the monasteries, and the right of the crown to appoint ecclesiastical officials.

Among Henry VIII's appointments to office in the Anglican Church was Thomas Cranmer (1489-1556), who served as the archbishop of Canterbury from 1533 to 1555. In order to regularize the Anglican Church, he wrote the *Ten Articles*, in which baptism, the Eucharist, and penance were recognized as sacraments. Through this document, Cranmer attempted to reconcile the radical Protestant and conservative factions among the church reformers. In his *Book of Common Prayer* (1549), he attempted to create a standard form of religious service, incorporating ideas promulgated by the various parties of church reformers. For one faction, though, the reforms did not go far enough.

The Church of England grew rapidly in the years following Henry's death with the exception of a period under Queen Mary I, who briefly restored the Roman Catholic Church before her half-sister, Elizabeth I, reestablished Anglican Protestantism as the state religion. During Catholic Mary's reign, a Scottish Protestant theologian, John Knox (c. 1514-1572), was forced into exile. In Geneva, he met John Calvin and studied the writings of the Reformation theologian. From his study of continental Protestantism, Knox developed his own version of a reformed liturgy. Upon returning to Scotland, John Knox led the Scottish Protestant nobles in creating a reformed church, called the Kirk, which is a Presbyterian church because it was governed not by a king or any head of state but rather by a group of elders.

In 1553, during the reign of Queen Mary, Thomas Cranmer and other prominent Protestants were scooped up and charged with treason. Cranmer himself escaped immediate execution and was held in prison long enough to make several recantations of his heretical writings, in particular, agreeing to submit to the authority of the queen and recognizing the pope as the head of the church. Despite the rule of Catholic canon law that those who recanted heresy should be spared execution, he was burned at the stake in 1556.

The conflicts between the kings who were sympathetic to Protestantism and those sympathetic to the papacy were, in many cases, not attributable to abstruse theological differences. For example, Holy Roman Emperor Charles V (r. 1519-1556) was suspected by Pope Clement VII (papacy 1523-1534) of secretly planning to usurp power over the Catholic Church in Italy by deposing the pope and instituting secular leadership. The pope allied the papacy with King Francis I of France (r. 1515-1547), from whom he obtained military support. The German troops of the Holy Roman emperor and his Spanish allies defeated the French Army in Italy. With funds running low, the German and Spanish troops were forced to forgo payment for their service. In 1527, the Germans mutinied, then marched to Rome, where they breached the city walls and overran the Swiss Guard in the Vatican. This sacking of Rome was intended to provide the soldiers with much-needed loot. The pope himself escaped to the Castel Sant'Angelo while the invading soldiers rampaged around the capital, stealing what they could from churches, monasteries, palaces, and shrines. They murdered between 6,000 and 12,000 citizens. Many of the mutinous soldiers were followers of Luther, who himself did not support an outright war against the papacy.

When Clement VII bought his freedom with a healthy amount of ransom, the Catholic Church, with its dependency on the papal court in Rome, was rocked to its foundation. The population of Rome declined precipitously as the influence of the Vatican declined. Emperor Charles V came to have considerable influence over church affairs, although he did not claim as Henry VIII did in England to be the head of the Christian Church. He refused the pope's request to engage in a holy war to unify Christian Europe and instead left the matter to the pope himself. Clement VII, fearing political consequences in a Europe with warring secular kings and contending religious factions, did not call a council to unify Catholics in contending with rising Protestant rebellions.

The decades-long instability of the Catholic Church in the first half of the 16th century fostered the growth of Protestantism in the form of the Church of England and the Church of Scotland. On the continent, the number of Anabaptists, Lutherans, and Calvinists grew exponentially. The threat to the dominance of the Catholic Church did not go unrecognized. A council composed of members of the hierarchy of the Catholic Church was convened at Trent in northern Italy (1545-1563). Its purpose was to formally condemn the various heresies propagated by sects of the Protestant faith. In doing so, it was necessary for the church to clarify its doctrines by establishing the accepted canon of biblical texts and defining original sin, salvation, the Eucharist, and the veneration of saints. All of these had come under siege in one form or another by Protestant theologians. The organization of a church council called and presided over by the papacy had been rejected by Martin Luther. He accepted only the authority of the secular state in moderating discussions of matters in the church.

After a number of failed efforts to convene a council that would have included prelates from around Europe and prominent Protestant dissenters, the Council of Trent was arranged to be held in a city controlled by a prince-bishop under the Holy Roman emperor. Over the various sessions of the council, the papacy was represented by legates. No popes attended. During the second series of meetings, from 1551 to 1552, Protestants were invited to address the council. Lutherans, who were denied a vote, requested a discussion of points of disagreement and demanded that bishops be released from their oaths of allegiance to the pope. This failed, and any notion of cooperation or reconciliation between Protestants and Catholics vanished. The officials of the church charged with examining the Catholic faith did not make any changes to the system of the sale of indulgences and the veneration of saints and relics. Among the decrees of the council was that the Vulgate Bible (late 4th-century Latin translation) was confirmed as the only authoritative text of the Holy Scriptures. This flew in the face of those who held that translations of the Bible into the vernacular tongues of Europe were essential to making the Word of God available to everyone. At the Council of Trent, the importance of the seven sacraments was reaffirmed. The Jesuits were the major force at the third installment of the Council of Trent, which was held between 1562 and 1563. The reforms of the Council of Trent were ratified by Pope Pius IV (papacy 1559-1569) and were made known to all Catholics in a papal bull. Those who contravened the bull were subject to excommunication. The Breviary, the Missal, and the Vulgate Bible were sanctioned as official church documents. An index of prohibited books was also established.

While the Council of Trent was transacting its business in strengthening the Catholic Church in opposition to the growing number of Protestant believers, there were prolonged wars in France between the Catholics and Protestant Huguenots, who were Calvinists. Claimants to the succession of the royal throne faced off as adherents of the two Christian sects. The troubles began during the reign of the humanist-tending Francis I (r. 1515-1547). Catholic humanist theologians adopted a rigorous method of understanding the scriptures in their original languages. The Catholic faith was propagated through printed books published by the burgeoning book business, as was the Protestant faith, whose anticlerical stance spread with the publications of Lutheran and Calvinist texts. Francis's successor, Henry II (r. 1547-1559), saw an increase in the persecution of the Protestants who, by royal edict, were banned from public worship. By 1562, the animosity with the Huguenots, who counted among their number a good share of the French nobility, came to a boil. The Protestants forcefully assumed control of major cities in France, establishing zones of protection for their fellows. Accusations of hostilities on both sides flew back and forth until anti-Protestant mobs attacked Paris in 1572, initiating a five-day massacre. The violence spread throughout France, where it is estimated that as many as 10,000 Huguenot men, women, and children were killed. The wars between the Huguenots and the

Catholics continued until the end of the 16ᵗʰ century when, in 1598, King Henry IV (r. 1589-1610) issued the Edict of Nantes, which was a kind of truce between the warring factions of Christianity in France.

Among the most active in contributing to the rebirth of the Catholic faith at the time of the Council of Trent were members of the Society of Jesus, also known as Jesuits. Founded by Ignatius of Loyola (1491-1556) and a group of like-minded friends in 1540, the Jesuit order was dedicated to the propagation of the gospel through evangelical missionary work and education in colleges, seminaries, and schools founded by the order. This work was, according to the Jesuit motto, "for the greater glory of God." In the constitution of the order, it was made clear that the Jesuits were to practice absolute self-denial and submit to the authority of the pope and the hierarchy of the church.

It was primarily through the work of the Jesuits that the Catholic faith was spread throughout the newly discovered world beyond Europe. One of Ignatius's Spanish companions in the founding of the Jesuit order, Francis Xavier (1506-1552), became the first of the Jesuit missionaries. Requested by King John of Portugal (r. 1521-1557) to strengthen Christianity in the new Portuguese territories in India, Francis traveled first to the Portuguese colony in Mozambique and then sailed to Goa. In Goa, the Jesuit priest set about providing education for the Portuguese children, establishing a college to act as a seminary for the instruction of new priests. Francis established many churches and worked to bring the fallen Christians in the region into the fold once again. Francis, always a restless missionary, traveled to Japan in 1549, where, due to language difficulties and local opposition to missionary work, he failed to win many converts. Back in Goa, Francis organized a small delegation to China. However, he died on the verge of entering China in 1552. About a quarter-century later, Jesuits became established in the Portuguese colony of Macau. It became clear that if missionary work was to proceed in China, it was necessary for Jesuits to speak Chinese. The training of young missionaries was accomplished at the newly founded Saint Paul Jesuit College in Macau. Despite changes in the Chinese imperial dynasty, which instituted the official closure of the country to Christians, the Jesuits made inroads among the Chinese, and by the mid-17th century, there was some travel by Chinese Jesuits to Europe.

Quite distinct from the Chinese missions, where the goal was to convert educated Taoists and Buddhists, Jesuit activity in the Americas was connected with pacifying the indigenous people as waves of avaricious European traders and pillagers flowed inland from the sea.

The Jesuits arrived in Peru in 1571 and worked hand in hand with the Spanish exploiters of the silver mines at Potosí in converting the indigenous people so that they would be peaceful slaves. After Hernán Cortés (1485-1547) laid waste to central Mexico between 1519 and 1521, with Spanish priests in his train to minister to his bloodthirsty band of conquistadors, the colony was quickly occupied by Christian missionaries. The Franciscan Diego de Landa Calderón (1524-1579), who became the archbishop of Yucatán, did his best to rid his part of the colony of indigenous religions by instigating an inquisition, during which 27 Maya books and 5,000 Maya cult images were burned. He imprisoned and tortured many Maya dignitaries as well. Landa paved the way for Jesuit missionaries in Latin America.

In Mexico, after 1572, the Jesuits quickly established themselves, converting the indigenous peoples, building churches, and creating schools and Christian communities. In North America, the Jesuits arrived on the heels of French explorers and settlers. The first Jesuit mission was established at Penobscot Bay in 1609, and from then on, more and more Jesuits arrived to preach the gospel to the Native Americans. A seminary was opened near Quebec City to teach indigenous peoples the French language and the precepts of

Christianity. These native scholars would go out into the hinterland and assist Jesuits at their remote missions. Later communities, also known as reductions, which were formed by the Jesuits for the collective settlement of indigenous peoples, began to dot the landscape along the Saint Lawrence.

The work of the Jesuits of converting the natives of the lands in Asia and America came to an abrupt halt when the European nations expelled the Jesuits from their dominions. The first to do so were the Portuguese. In the Portuguese royal court in 1759, a dispute arose over colonial sovereignty in South America. Since the Jesuits had such an avid interest in their several missions in the Western Hemisphere, they did not quietly accept interference in their goals. They were accused of interfering in political and secular affairs. As a result, the Jesuits in Portuguese-controlled areas of South America were deported. The supposed ringleader of Jesuit malfeasance in Brazil, Gabriel Malagrida (1689–1761), was imprisoned in Portugal. He was accused of high treason and executed after his appearance before the Court of Inquisition for his heretical writings. In France, the Jesuits ran afoul of the reformist Jansenists, who persecuted them in the French Parliament, claiming that they were immoral and had fallen into theological error. The constitution of the Society of Jesus was revoked in 1764. In New France, with the defeat of the French by the British in 1759, the Jesuit missions gradually declined. When the Spanish reorganized their empire, they suppressed the Jesuits, who may or may not have interfered in the king's government. They were first expelled from Spain by a royal edict in 1767, and those Jesuits who did not disavow their membership in the order were shipped to Italy. In Mexico, the Jesuits were removed from their sixteen missions. The properties of the Jesuits, which were, in reality, wealthy haciendas in which the indigenous peoples were to be "civilized" and Christianized, were auctioned off, and in some parts of Mexico, the Jesuit stations were repopulated with Franciscan friars. By 1773,

Pope Clement XIV (papacy 1769–1774) formalized the dissolution of the Jesuit order.

In England, the trajectory of the evolution of the Christian faith was far from consistent. Henry VIII's dissolution of the Catholic Church, the distribution of church properties to members of his loyal faction, and the long reign of Elizabeth I allowed for the firm establishment of the Protestant Anglican Church as a state institution. However, it was only shortly after the conversion of the nation to Anglicanism that Protestantism became fractured. A large portion of the faithful Protestants tended toward the kind of pietism and church governance practiced in Presbyterian Scotland. These Puritans placed their hopes on the ascension of James VI of Scotland (who ruled England from 1603 to 1625 as James I) to rid the Anglican Church of what they called popish practices. This included the use of the sign of the cross at baptism and bowing when the name of Jesus was uttered. They advocated strict adherence to rules marking the Sabbath and the reduction of music in church services. King James I convened a church conference, where it was affirmed that the governance of the Anglican Church would be a hierarchy, not the Presbyterian system of governance by presbyters. The most lasting of James I's reforms was the retranslation of the Bible by a committee of theologians and church officials. The final say in the text of the new Bible remained in the hands of James I himself. The King James Version became the accepted text of the Bible for centuries thereafter among English-speaking Protestants.

The ascension of Charles I to the throne of England in 1625 increased the strain between the official Anglican Church and Parliament, which was dominated by Puritans. Under the auspices of the king, conservative Anglican ecclesiastics managed to have it mandated that church services be more formal with an emphasis on the sacraments and ceremony. In other words, it was to be more Catholic-like. This raised the ire of those who advocated simplicity in worship. The imposition of a new Anglican prayer book in Scotland, which was a hotbed of Presbyterianism, led to revolts that Charles I attempted unsuccessfully to put down with his military. When the king convened a new Parliament in London, the members themselves revolted and imprisoned the archbishop of Canterbury, who they accused of infecting the state with popish religion. A civil war broke out between the forces of Parliament, which was under the leadership of Oliver Cromwell. Charles I was executed, and the Puritans under Cromwell assumed national leadership. In the last phase of the English Civil War, Cromwell invaded Ireland and massacred a huge number of Catholics at Drogheda in 1649. Cromwell, who had done his best to purify religion in England with the sacking and destruction of any remaining ancient images in English churches, established a rule with some measure of religious tolerance for Protestant dissenters. Minor sects were allowed to exist. Among them were the Levellers, who pushed for a more egalitarian society; the Diggers, who advocated communal land ownership; and the Ranters, who were opposed to most traditional Christian doctrines. The number of Baptist congregations grew during this time. Particularly attractive to the common people was the Baptist belief in adult rebaptism. Under Cromwell, Catholics were persecuted, but the Jews who had been expelled from England in 1290 were allowed, indeed encouraged, to resettle. Cromwell's government eventually crumbled, and the monarchy was restored under Charles II (r. 1660–1685).

The rate of reform in England was not sufficiently swift for some of the Puritans. During the reign of James I, some fled to the Netherlands and then sailed off to North America in 1620, where they founded a colony. The rate of emigration picked up with every royal edict that promoted high Anglican religious services and adherence to the ecclesiastical hierarchy. The colony of Puritans, who settled around Massachusetts Bay, became official when a royal charter was granted to John Winthrop in 1629. It is said that while aboard the ship crossing the Atlantic, Winthrop observed, "We shall be as a city upon a hill, and the eyes of all people are upon us." This has become a cliché in the American understanding of the founding of the United States and the position of the nation in the world, even today. The new Puritans believed in a covenant between God and man. Those who adhered to the faith were expected to undergo a dramatic expression of conversion. The so-called freedom of religion that the Puritans sought in America evolved into intolerance of all non-believers. This was exemplified in the Salem witch trials in the late 17th century.

In the period of the Reformation and Counter-Reformation, European church architecture and furnishings underwent a major change. When the new Protestant denominations came to predominate in a country or region, the easiest way to acquire a vessel in which to worship was to appropriate an existing Catholic church. This was done in England, where the old cathedral churches and abundant parish churches were, with few minor modifications, such as the reduction of painted and sculptural images, put into service as Anglican churches. On the continent, more energetic transformations occurred. For example, in 1566, in the Low Countries, *Beeldenstorm* ("image storm" or "statue storm") broke out. Protestant mobs thronged the churches, monasteries, and convents of Antwerp and destroyed Catholic images and demolished some buildings entirely. It was reported that the cathedral in Antwerp "looked like a hell, with above 10,000 torches burning, and such a noise as if heaven and earth had got together, with falling of images and beating down of costly works." The mobs moved on to Amsterdam, where a spate of iconoclasm followed. When a Catholic church was purged of its Catholic images, it could be reused as an austere Protestant house of worship.

The Catholic counter to this was to add to the panoply of earlier churches by erecting magnificent edifices and decorating them with didactic art that clearly told the story of the faith. The style of the new visual art, both sculptures and paintings, involved dynamic and dramatic representations of the stories of Christ and the saints that could be comprehended by everyone. Grand buildings, such as St. Peter's Basilica in Rome, were erected in the 16th-century Renaissance style. Like the literary culture of the period, this style was centered on revived Roman ideas. This bold response to ancient culture symbolized a new beginning for the Catholic Church and also affirmed its long history.

By the start of the 17th century, by which time the Protestant church had a wide following, the Catholic Counter-Reformation was in high gear. Starting in Italy, a new form of ecclesiastical architecture was introduced primarily by the Jesuits. It was the decorative and theatrical Baroque style, which, with its intricate surface detailing and capacity, surprised and inspired awe among the people. Baroque church building spread quickly from Italy into Spain, Portugal, and France, and it was transported to their colonial dominions as well. With high painted ceilings and pleasantly rounded arches, the interior of Baroque churches were ideal places for the presentation of emotional and dramatic sacred music, vocal, instrumental, and organ pieces by the likes of the Italian Claudio Monteverdi (1567–1643), the Danish-German Dietrich Buxtehude (c. 1637–1707), and Johann Pachelbel (1653–1706). In the Protestant churches, music also played a significant role in the spiritual uplifting expected by congregations in their worship. Martin Luther was a writer of hymns, and the first Lutheran hymnal dates from 1524. He believed that music in the church should be "accorded the greatest honor and a place next to theology." His liberal approach to music was countered by the leader of the Reformation in Switzerland, Huldrych Zwingli, who rejected all forms of music in worship. He not only had all works of art removed from the church but, in occupying formerly Catholic houses of worship, he also instructed that organs be removed and destroyed. According to Zwingli, music and art were promoters of self-indulgence. John Calvin, on the other hand, liked simple songs in worship and was a proponent of children's choirs. In England, the Anglican Church made use of music by the likes of the composer William Byrd (c. 1539-1623), who wrote sacred music for the Protestant church before becoming a Roman Catholic sometime in the 1570s.

Chapter 5 – The 18th-Century Church

The Christian Church began as a collection of the faithful who practiced their religion in different ways from one part of the Roman Empire to another. Unity of the faith was achieved by Christians submitting to the church hierarchy under the leadership of the pope. This unity was threatened periodically up to the time of the Reformation; however, it was after the floodgates of dissent were opened by Luther, Zwingli, Calvin, and others that the Christian Church became an array of countless sects and denominations.

In North America, the sway of not only the Catholics but also the fervent Puritans crumbled as waves of new immigrants brought contending ideas into the colonies. In New England, the power of fervent Puritanism slowly diminished in the colonies to be replaced by distinct Protestant factions. The Congregationalists, so-called because each congregation was sovereign or autonomous, abandoned the severity of Calvinism and based their religion on Enlightenment principles, looking to a rational understanding of God. Their theology was situated between Presbyterianism and Baptists. Distinct from the Congregationalists were "Old Calvinists," who continued to adhere to rigid forms of worship and behavior.

The New England Protestant sects established in the 1730s and 1740s took place during what is known as the Great Awakening or New Birth. Generally, the New England Great Awakening, which passed through several waves of intensity, involved a rejection of rituals and ceremonies in the church and focused more on individual spiritual conviction and the goal of redemption. The First Great Awakening during the 1730s was carried forth by several energetic Protestants of various denominations. At its core, the Great Awakening depended on the work of itinerant preachers who led the movement of evangelical revivalism. One of the most influential preachers in the Great Awakening was George Whitefield (1714-1770). He was among the founders of Methodism in England and a leader in the evangelical movement. Whitefield traveled to America in 1749, where he preached at several evangelical revivals. In the audience at one of these in Philadelphia was Benjamin Franklin, who said that Whitefield changed the behavior of his audience "from being thoughtless or indifferent about religion" to one that was devout "so that one could not walk through the town in an evening without hearing psalms sung in different families of every street." On one of his several preaching missions to America, Whitefield was one of the first preachers in America to address slaves.

The popular religion espoused by Whitefield and the evangelists crisscrossing the American colonies was quite separate from the pursuit of theological truths in academic institutions. In the 18th century, Christian dogma, both Protestant and Roman Catholic, became a subject of intense scrutiny by Enlightenment scholars. At the base of lively debates was the serious intent of understanding the message of the Christian faith without the incursion of the myth and legend that was anathema, or so the scholars believed, for any thinking rational man. The writers of the Age of Enlightenment worked to bring light to Christian dogma by employing rational thought and the kind of scrutiny common to students of the new scientific method. The project of purging the Christian faith from centuries of accretions of myth and legend was a contentious and often dangerous undertaking. It is important to recognize that ancient beliefs, such as the stories of the early Christian saints and martyrs, were ingrained in the daily life of Christians, particularly those of the peasant class. Their lives, even when they migrated to cities and became burghers, were defined by religion. The hours of work and days of work were established by a Christian calendar. Further, for many, it was the church that taxed the populace in the form of tithes paid as rent for farmlands owned by the church.

Frederick William I, King of Prussia (r. 1713-1740), ruled over a population in Germany who were mainly Lutherans of the Pietist persuasion. As such, they believed in strict adherence to the biblical doctrine of living a simple Christian life revolving around individual piety. The Pietist movement was founded by the Lutheran theologian Philipp Spener (1635-1705). He advocated seminary schools in which the professors set an example of Christian humility. His stance in respect to the study of the scriptures was followed at the University of Halle (founded in 1694), where under the intellectual leadership of August Hermann Francke (1663-1727), students were taught to study the Bible so that they understood the text as it was intended to be understood by the Holy Spirit. This required that students acquire knowledge in a number of ancient languages in order to tease the true meaning from the original biblical texts. As well as promoting theological studies, the Pietists directed their energy to founding Christian charities. King Frederick William was a staunch supporter of the Pietist movement, standing with them in their efforts to remove Christian Wolff (1679-1754), a rationalist scholar, from the faculty of Halle. Wolff had suggested in his writings that God was not a prerequisite for moral reasoning. He promulgated this idea in his book *On the Practical Philosophy of the Chinese*, in which he attempted to show that Confucianism could elicit moral truths without reference to the Christian God. Wolff, as an ardent Enlightenment philosopher, professed a desire to base theological truths on mathematically certain evidence.

Two of the students at the University of Halle were selected to serve on the king of Denmark's mission to propagate the faith in India. They traveled to southern India, translated the Bible into Tamil, and established a charity school and a seminary for missionaries. German Lutheran Pietists from Halle also served as missionaries throughout eastern Europe, pushing into Moravia, Bohemia, and Peter the Great's (r. 1682-1725) Russia. The missionaries from Halle, who numbered some sixty students, were provided with Bibles printed by the Canstein Bible Institute (founded by Karl Hildebrand von Canstein, 1667-1719) for distribution to their ever-increasing flocks of Poles and Czechs.

The successes of the Pietist movement in Germany and abroad may have been owing to the power of radical Pietists to appeal to the common folk. Among the founders of the radical strain of Pietism was a German philosopher of the previous century. Jakob Böhme (1575-1624) wrote extensively on the subjects of sin, evil, and redemption. He proposed that the fall of man was a necessary stage in the evolution of the universe. He believed this was true due to a mystical vision he had in which it was made clear to him by God that to obtain redemption and to see God, man must first go through hell. Böhme's mystical approach to the divine was highly influential on several groups of Pietist Protestants, such as Johannes Kelpius's (1667-1708) Society of the Woman in the Wilderness, which held that the Book of Revelation predicted that there was a place in the wilderness where a heavenly kingdom existed. The Christian mystic Kelpius and his followers thus sailed to America and settled in Pennsylvania, where they expected to greet the end of times in 1694 with the advent of the heavenly Kingdom of Jerusalem. Like all Christian millenarist sects who expect a radical change in society after a cataclysm, such as the Black Death, the followers of Kelpius did not see the end of the world in 1694.

Nevertheless, his acolytes patiently lived on in celibacy in caves and small cells as the Hermits or Mystics of Wissahickon. Since this Christian sect was celibate, it did not survive into modern times.

Not all Pietists were as radical nor as doomed to failure as Kelpius. Philipp Spener, the founder of the Pietist movement, became the mentor of Nicolaus Ludwig von Zinzendorf (1700–1760). Zinzendorf gave refuge on his estate to religious refugees from Moravia called the *Unitas Fratrum* (the Unity of Brethren), who traced their spiritual lineage back to the pre-Reformation John Hus. Zinzendorf's Brethren built a village they called Herrnhut, or "the Lord's watch." At religious services, the Holy Spirit surged through the congregation in what is called the "Moravian Pentecost." The Moravians became particularly occupied with missionary work. They were the first large-scale Protestant missionary movement. Two Moravians went to the West Indies in 1732, one to Greenland in 1733, and another to Georgia in the same year. Over the years, they were followed by many faithful missionaries who brought Christianity to the wilds of North and South America, the Arctic, Africa, and the Far East. In the Americas, the Moravian Brethren worked primarily with the indigenous peoples. To this end, they used the earliest translation of a Bible into a North American First Nations language. This Bible, *Mamusse Wunneetupanatamwe Up Biblum God*, translate into Algonquian, was published in 1663 by the Massachusetts Puritan John Eliot (1604–1690).

The disarray within the Holy Roman Empire with states vying for independence came to an end with the rise of Frederick II, also known as Frederick the Great, and his defeat of the Austrian Hapsburgs in 1740–42. Dominance in central Europe was won by Frederick the Great (r. 1740–1786), whose court in Berlin promised an efficient and humane environment for the evolution of the Christian Church comprised of the Catholic faith and a plethora of Protestant denominations. In Bavaria, the Catholic

Enlightenment clerics sought to end the dominance of the Jesuits associated with the University of Ingolstadt. Another group of Bavarian dissidents formed a Masonic-like group of like-minded individuals who styled themselves as the Bavarian Order of Illuminati. They were accused of harboring anti-Christian sentiments and were banned in Bavaria in 1784.

Frederick, who was always quite liberal-minded when it came to religion, removed the ban on Christian Wolff, who then returned to the University of Halle to teach. It was at Halle that a group of scholars attempted to reconcile the new thinking of the Enlightenment with Christian thought. Prominent among them were the Neologians, who worked to accommodate the scientific and reasoned thinking of the Enlightenment with Christian theology. These scholars believed that the truths revealed by reason were not incompatible with the revealed divine truths of the Bible. The liberal-thinking Neologians soon had a university that was sympathetic to their new way of looking at Christianity. In 1737, the University of Göttingen was founded to prepare students for work in the growing civil service of the Prussian state. At Halle, the new biblical criticism was also accepted. Free investigation of the Bible untied to the presuppositions of scholastic orthodoxy and the infallibility of religious texts was encouraged. It was proposed by Johann Salomo Semler (1725-1791), the most influential German philosopher of the time, that there was a distinction between religion and theology and between the "Word of God" and the "Holy Scripture." He proposed that the scriptures, or rather Jewish history, were written by taking into account all the faulty views of contemporaries (ancient Jews), which means this was thus not the eternally true Word of God.

The challenge in reconciling history and revelation for the scholars of the Enlightenment is clearly stated in the writings of Johann Philipp Gabler (1753-1826), a professor at Nuremberg. In a lecture entitled "An Oration on the Proper Distinction between

Biblical and Dogmatic Theology and the Specific Objectives of Each," he said that he would develop a methodological guide for those who "aspired to a solid understanding of divine matters" and "to obtain a firm and certain hope of salvation." For him, practical reason delivered universal truths of theology that were historical in origin. He believed that the Holy Scripture could contain myths that stemmed from primitive cultures. From these myths, the diligent scholar could then sift out universal truths.

The freedom that biblical scholars enjoyed in their exploration of the Christian faith in Frederick's Prussia was usurped by many hack writers who, under the guise of enlightened rationalism, attacked such things as miracles and fabulous events related in the Bible. This led to the institution of a censorship edict promulgated by Frederick the Great's successor, his nephew Frederick William II (r. 1786-1797). All theological writing was subject to state approval. The immediate goal was to stem the flow of writings and preaching by the followers of the Italian theologian Fausto Sozzini, also known as Faustus Socinus (1539-1604). His school of Christian thought, known as Socinianism, came from the believers in the Radical Reformation. Socinians rejected orthodox notions of God's knowledge, the Trinity, the divinity of Christ, and the concept of salvation. Socinians formed the Minor Reformed Church of Poland and the Unitarian Church of Transylvania. These Socinian denominations had a nontrinitarian Christology, and they also rejected the doctrine of original sin and the absolute omniscience of God. The Unitarian Church of Transylvania became subject to persecution. The most famous martyr for the nontrinitarian faith was Katarzyna Weiglowa, or Katherine Weigel (c. 1460-1539). She was executed in Kraków after converting to Judaizing nontrinitarianism. She refused to recognize Christ as the Son of God. Katarzyna Weiglowa is considered to be a martyr by both Unitarians and Jews. In the 18th century, Unitarianism spread to England, where the first Unitarian church was founded in London in 1774. In America, the first clergyman to call himself a Unitarian was James Freeman (1759-1835). His preaching at Stone Chapel in Boston in 1784 on the Socinian doctrine of the Godhead won over the congregation, which means Stone Chapel might be considered the first Unitarian church in America.

In Sweden, catastrophic defeats by the Russians and the loss of Baltic territories eventually turned the monarch away from absolutist tendencies. The new Age of Liberty (1719-1772) permitted German Pietists to infiltrate the Lutheran Church in Sweden. Among the liberal thinkers enjoying the freedom to consider heterodox ideas was Emanuel Swedenborg (1688-1772). Swedenborg was a scientist who had a spiritual awakening through revelation. He was told by Jesus Christ, who he met in a vision, to write *The Heavenly Doctrine*, a 1758 account of his visit to heaven and hell where, apart from Christ, he was afforded the opportunity to converse with angels and demons. The interlude of religious openness continued under King Gustavus III (r. 1772-1792), but he established Lutheranism as the basis of government and established his constitutional control over the Lutheran Church.

During the 18th century, England saw the rise of a Protestant sect that was somewhat less lofty than those that came out of German university theology schools. The leader of the largest English sect of dissenters was John Wesley (1703-1791), who was an ordained Anglican priest. He joined the "Holy Club," a society founded by his brother Charles. Among its members was George Whitefield, who would soon become an itinerant preacher in England and America. John Wesley served for two years as a priest in Savannah in Georgia Colony. On returning to London, he joined a group of Moravian Christians. Wesley experienced what he called an evangelical conversion and set out to establish his own evangelical ministry. While traveling and preaching outdoors around England and Ireland, he helped groups organize in which, as Christians, they accepted personal accountability, committed to discipleship, and offered religious instruction. He taught that it was through faith that a Christian could be transformed into the likeness of Christ. Inward and outward holiness could be obtained by those who let the love of God directly into their hearts. Wesley's evangelical approach to broadcasting the Word of God was accepted by the orthodox Anglican Church. It was only after he died that those who practiced his method of living this kind of Christian life, Methodists, became the object of persecution and were forced to establish themselves as belonging to a separate denomination.

The greatest crisis faced by the Christian Church in Europe occurred in the twilight years of the 18th century. After the French Revolution had succeeded in upending almost all vestiges of the royal government of France, the revolutionary government developed policies for the dechristianization of the country. The Catholic Church was first attacked for its wealth and power over the now-defunct royal government, and confiscated church properties were sold at public auction. At first, the clergy were stripped of their rights and made employees of the state, which means they were subject to election by their parishioners. This flew in the face of papal authority, as did the legalization of divorce in 1792. In the fall of 1792, anti-clericalism became violent. Eventually, the church was completely suppressed, and all its properties were nationalized. Thirty thousand priests were exiled, and many more were murdered. Everything Christian came under fire. The calendar was recalculated so that *Anno domini* was replaced by the year since the fall of the Bastille in 1789. Any mention of the Sabbath, days of saints, or Christian festival days were obliterated from the calendar. Some of the churches taken over by the government were renamed Temples of Reason. The Temples of Reason were houses for the celebration of the state-sponsored atheistic religion called the Cult of Reason. After a very short period of dominance, the Cult of Reason was officially replaced by the Cult of the Supreme Being. It was only with the rise of Napoleon Bonaparte (1769–1821) that the two anti-Christian cults were banned. Napoleon was pragmatic when it came to the Christian Church. He understood that secular power in Europe depended to some extent on the acquiescence of the Catholic Church. It was in this spirit that he invited Pope Pius VII (papacy 1800–1823) to bless his coronation as the emperor of France in 1804.

Chapter 6 – The Church in the 19th Century

The godless French Revolution had a resounding impact on both the Protestant and Catholic churches in Europe and abroad. In England, Edmund Burke (1729-1797), an astute observer of political affairs, railed against the French destruction of civil and religious society. He opined that it was Trinitarian Christianity that formed the basis of society and that its destruction by French revolutionaries presaged the collapse of civilization. For Burke, it was clear that church and state were intimately bound in an indissoluble union. Burke's notions were opposed by writers who proposed that the rights of man should prevail in civil society. Works such as Mary Wollstonecraft's *A Vindication of the Rights of Men* (1790) and *A Vindication of the Rights of Woman* (1792) strongly supported the intent of French notions of inherent rights. Many in England feared that if the nation became infected by French ideas, the authority of the Crown, Parliament, and Anglicanism, as well as numerous dissenting Protestant sects, would be put in jeopardy. The Methodists, for example, in a series of conferences in the 1790s, affirmed the proposition that the faithful should submit to the authority of the king; otherwise, a revolution like that in France would destroy religion entirely. The same conflict between religion and the state arose in the new United States, where admirers of the French Revolution, like Thomas Paine (1737-1809), the author of the *Rights of Man* (1791), and Thomas Jefferson, the third president of the United States (in office from 1801 to 1809), questioned the truth of the Christian faith. Paine wrote that the Bible "is a book of lies, wickedness and blasphemy; What is it the Bible teaches us? Rapine, cruelty, and murder." He said that his own mind was his church. Jefferson, being a rational Enlightenment scholar, did not go so far. Along with the other framers of the Constitution in the First Amendment, he ensured that the freedom of religion was guaranteed and that the state was prohibited from passing laws establishing a national religion.

A kind of peace was negotiated between the Catholic Church and the new French Republic with a concordat negotiated between Napoleon Bonaparte and the pope in 1801. It ensured that the Roman Catholic Church, Jews, and adherents of Protestant sects were given the right to freely worship in France and that the Catholic Church would not be reestablished as the state religion. The peace between the papacy and Napoleon did not last long. Shortly after his coronation, Napoleon's armies invaded the Papal States in Italy and captured the pope, who was taken to France and imprisoned. He remained a captive until the eve of Napoleon's defeat at Waterloo in 1815.

Napoleon's conquest of Europe and his attack on the tsar of Russia, while not lasting, had the effect of enhancing, at least on the surface, the alliance of the Christian states. After the final defeat of Napoleon at the Battle of Waterloo in 1815, Tsar Alexander I of Russia (r. 1801-1825) formed a Holy Alliance with Emperor Francis I of Austria (r. 1804-1835) and the King Frederick William III of Prussia (r. 1797-1840). The three monarchs agreed to follow Christianity and its principles in restoring their kingdoms after the depredations of Napoleon. The same kind of motivation was behind the restoration of the Jesuits by the pope in 1814. In France, there was a movement to restore the credibility of Christianity as a guiding faith for mankind by several apologists, among whom was François-René de Chateaubriand (1768–1848), who wrote that, "Christianity is perfect; men are imperfect. Now, a perfect consequence cannot spring from an imperfect principle. Christianity, therefore, is not the work of men." This kind of thinking was to be highly influential in the slow regrowth of Catholicism in France.

The post-Napoleonic reorganization of Europe, which was accomplished by the ruling elite, led the lower-class citizenry to abandon any hopes of achieving rights like those promised by the French Revolution. For the most part, the status and economic conditions of the European lower classes declined with the rise of industrialism and the increasingly unequal distribution of wealth. Political treatises, such as Giuseppe Mazzini's (1805–1872) *An Essay on the Duties of Man Addressed to the Workingmen* (1844), advocated for the freedom of the lower classes from the arbitrary actions of the upper classes. Mazzini said that in achieving their rights, the workingman should turn to God rather than rely on godless revolutionaries.

The rise of political liberalism fomented in the now overcrowded cities of Europe, where poverty and disease proliferated, became tied to concepts of overthrowing the old order and, with it, some of the old order thinking of the Christian Church. In Greece, the orthodox Christians rebelled against their Islamic Ottoman overlords. This push for independence and an ideal of equality in a democratic government became a clarion call throughout Europe. A constitutional monarchy was established in France, but shortly after his coronation, the second Bourbon king, Charles X (r. 1824–1830), presided over the restoration of the Roman Catholic Church as the French state church. Ultra conservatives rose to prominence in the French bureaucracy, so much so that it was observed at the time that "one talks of nothing but bishops, priests, monks, Jesuits, convents and seminaries." Draconian regulations that were intended to ensure the purity of the church were met with opposition, and an uprising in 1830 forced the king to abdicate and forced the people to establish a new monarchy. The bourgeoisie soon rose to prominence, as did opposition liberals who actively pursued a concept of universal freedom. Although insurgents in 1832 failed to dislodge the ruling class, the cause of ending the exploitation of the poor and the brotherhood of mankind grew among the French lower classes, who often looked to the Christian Church for justification of their demands.

Europe became embroiled in social unrest. This was particularly important in regions that had become highly industrialized. Many of those advocating for the rights of the workingmen believed that it was only through the Christian faith that any sort of reform could be accomplished. In France, Henri Comte de Saint-Simon (1760–1825) attacked the liberal thinkers of his time who, he said, only wanted political changes so that they could scoop up more power for themselves. It was only when the laboring classes achieved fair treatment and were the recipients of Christian benevolence that society could claim to be a brotherhood of man. It was always a conundrum whether the lower classes behaved in un-Christian-like ways because of deprivation or whether it was their depraved ways that landed them in positions of financial straits. William Wilberforce attempted to do something about the possibility that behavior led to poverty when he founded the Society for the Suppression of Vice (the former Proclamation Society Against Vice and Immorality) in England in the late 18th century. He intended to attack excessive drinking, blasphemy, lewdness, and the profanation of the Lord's Day. The idea was to get the fallen to attend church and mend their ways. Wilberforce, who also championed missionary work, would become a major advocate for the abolition of slavery, which led to the passing of the Slavery Abolition Act of

1833, thus ending the practice in most of the British Empire. Wilberforce is a great example of Christians in action against immorality and injustice in the 19th century.

The pan-European outbreak of insurgencies against the status quo in 1848 did very little to advance the utopian goal of Christian charity to all classes of men. The same can be said of the independence movements that swept across the Caribbean and Latin American colonies of France, Spain, and Portugal. The slave revolt in Haiti, which lasted from 1791 to 1804, resulted in the replacement of French autocratic rule with a similar but locally led autocracy. In Latin America, between 1808 and 1826, the same occurred with Spanish and Portuguese governments, which were replaced with new locally led dictatorships or pseudo-democracies. Essentially, the role of the church remained the same within the new states, as many of the insurgents were inspired by such Catholic leaders as Father Miguel Hidalgo y Costilla (1753–1811), who became a martyr in the Mexican Revolution. Still, many of the various newly independent states attempted to stem the authority of religion by passing and retracting anticlerical laws. An example of the complex relationship between church and state in Latin America is that of Argentina, or what was then known as the United Provinces of the Rió de la Plata. This was a revolutionary, locally led junta that won control of the Spanish colony in May 1810. The inquisition was suppressed, and the new government declared that the state would be "independent from any ecclesiastical authorities existing outside its territory." It was decided that although the official religion of Argentine would be Catholicism, the society itself should be secular and allow religious freedom. The president of the new republic would appoint bishops that the pope could then approve. In essence, the system as devised in Argentina in dealing with the Christian religion was one of threading the needle between what was desirable for liberals in a modern state and a pragmatic response to the history of the church.

The rapid industrialization of Europe in the 19th century changed the demographics of the continent. Vast numbers of peasants left the land and moved into cities. Living conditions in the suddenly expanding towns and cities were, in many cases, unhealthy, and the effects of poverty became obvious. Part of the government's solution was to hide the poor in neighborhoods, far from the homes of the entrepreneurial/proprietor classes. For many enterprises, they found that profits could be enlarged with increased productivity of the manual laborers, who were pressed to work harder and harder in often unsafe conditions. The culmination of industrialism and the mistreatment of the labor force was the publication of Karl Marx's (1818-1883) and Friedrich Engels's (1820-1895) pamphlet, *The Communist Manifesto* in 1848, the year of the European revolutions. They said that modern society evolved from a history of class struggles and that the solution to class inequity in a modern capitalist society was to replace it with socialism. This, coupled with the publication of Charles Darwin's (1809-1882) *On the Origin of Species* in 1859, ushered in a new era in Christian theological speculation and Christian social action.

Darwin's scientific approach flew in the face of revealed knowledge as understood by Christians. For those seeking objective truth based on empirical data, Darwin's theories had such influence that the general notion of Darwinian evolution was applied to social and political affairs and to the gradual development of civilization itself. It came to be believed that through modern science, what was truthful, right, and useful could be made known to mankind. God's providence in history fell by the wayside in the writings of such scholars as historian Leopold von Ranke (1795-1886), who established the modern notion of basing a narrative of history on primary sources. This was a complete departure from the idea that history was a chronology of the acts of God. At the same time, scholars of ethics, previously a division of theology, determined that natural ethics should be based on the scientific study of human evolution and not, as Christians had maintained, on the Word of

God. In an 1880 essay, Thomas Huxley (1825-1896), a great defender of Darwin, said that natural knowledge was the primary shaper of human life and that academics should pay more attention to science than classical studies.

Under normal circumstances, the writings of scientists were of interest to a small community of practitioners of natural and physical sciences. This was not true of Darwin's work, which was accessible to a large audience who eagerly consumed his observations. Of particular importance to Christians were Darwin's theories of evolution and the creation of species, which seemed to counter the story given in the Old Testament Book of Genesis that God had created everything in the universe and that what existed now was exactly as it was in the days of creation. In *The Descent of Man, and Selection in Relation to Sex*, published in 1871, Darwin caused a stir with the declaration that humans had evolved from lower forms of beings, such as apes. Even though, as a scientist, he did not hold with the literal truth of the creation story as given in Genesis, Darwin did believe that there was a "creator."

It seemed that in the 19th century, the world as Christians understood it was under assault from scientists and scholars in other fields of study. Further inroads against traditional religious beliefs were being made in the writings of philosophers. The challenge to traditional theology by modern philosophy is clear in writings such as those of Ludwig Feuerbach (1804-1872). In *The Essence of Christianity* (1841), he wrote that when we pray to God, we are not communicating with an essence beyond ourselves but are rather engaged in self-catharsis. This kind of statement was heretical for most Christians at the time, whether they be Protestant or Catholic. A contemporary German philosopher noted that science had destroyed the supernatural in Christianity. What were once held to be miraculous, inexplicable powers attributed to the spirits and God were all explicable by science. Metaphysical concepts of traditional religion were swept away in a mad rage for scientific rationalism.

The German philosopher Friedrich Nietzsche (1844-1900) famously declared God to be dead. By this, he meant not the literal death of God but the death of the concept of God as held by earlier theologians. According to Nietzsche, people in the modern world required new notions of morality and ethics, as well as the source for these, which he stated was not God. Nietzsche was a firm believer that no absolutes exist and dealt with all prior philosophy by the notion that "there are no facts, only interpretations."

The kind of speculation on religion that was coming from German philosophers was challenged by renewed debates on the dichotomy between revealed religion and the scientific method, on the importance of the trappings of Christian worship, and on the push and pull between contemplative spirituality and faith in action.

A movement, which was centered at Oxford University, arose among Anglicans for the restoration of traditions in the liturgy and theology. The Protestant preference for simplicity in church services, church governance, and ecclesiastical architecture and decoration had the effect of driving some, particularly the highly educated, to look backward, particularly to the Middle Ages when faith and the expression of it was a matter of simple piety enhanced by the trappings of the ecclesiastical environment. The Oxford Tractarian Movement, named after their publications, *Tracts for the Times* (published 1833-1841), promoted the revival of Roman Catholic-like liturgy in the Anglican Church. A prominent member of this group was an Anglican priest and theologian named John Henry Newman (1801-1890). He wrote, "Liberalism is the mistake of subjecting to human judgment those revealed doctrines which are in their nature beyond and independent of it, and of claiming to determine on intrinsic grounds the truth and value of propositions which rest for their reception simply on the external authority of the Divine Word." The rise of Protestant liberalism required the appropriate use of the historical-critical method in biblical studies. According to Newman, if one did not do this, it would lead to atheism. Newman's beliefs in the pre-Reformation theology of the Catholic Church were so strong that he eventually left the Oxford Movement and converted to Catholicism. He wrote extensively on his beliefs, most notably in *Apologia Pro Vita Sua* (1864), and he worked tirelessly to advance the cause of British and Irish Catholics who had only recently, in 1829, been emancipated from political and educational restrictions in the United Kingdom. The resurrection of traditional forms of worship proposed by the High Anglican members of the Oxford Movement and later the renewed British Catholic Church required decorations and congregational vessels that reflected the ancient traditions. These were provided by Roman Catholic architects and designers, such as August Welby Pugin (1812-1852), who determined that the Gothic style was the only one suitable for Christian churches. The Gothic Revival came to dominate ecclesiastical and secular architecture, particularly academic institutions, in Great Britain, her colonial empire, and America.

In Germany, similar discourses were conducted among academics to discover how to reconcile the traditions of Christianity and the needs of the modern world. The base of this discussion was how to understand the true meaning of the Holy Scriptures. The Protestant scholar Friedrich Daniel Ernst Schleiermacher (1768-1834), a one-time student and professor at Halle University, attempted to create an innovative system of ethics based on the careful study of the biblical texts. He set out to avoid rejecting religion based on reason, instead accepting one's feelings and intuitions, which preceded any rational construction of dogma. For Schleiermacher, religion embraced immediate feelings of the infinite. Belief tells us that there is existence beyond that of rational argument. Higher consciousness and religious experiences are essential components of theology. Using his advanced textual criticism, Schleiermacher wrote voluminously on the subject of the historical Jesus. To do this convincingly, it became of paramount importance to date the gospels. Schleiermacher was fortunate that, at the time, archaeology had become a scientific discipline in Germany, and more and more historical facts were emerging from excavations around the Mediterranean. Information of ancient cultures that could be applied to understanding the historical context of the Bible emerged from the work of intrepid archaeologists such Heinrich Schliemann (1822-1890) at Troy and Mycenae and Austen Henry Layard (1817-1894) at Nimrud and Nineveh.

With advancing scientific evidence emerging from archaeologist trenches around the Near East, it became more and more urgent that history and the Christian faith find some sort of meeting ground. This was very much like the urgency for reconciliation between Darwinian science and the Christian understanding of social conditions among the working classes. The rise of questions regarding whether dogmas in the Christian Church corresponded to the teachings of Jesus was essential to the work of many scholars, such as the Lutheran theologian Carl Gustav Adolf von Harnack (1851-1930). In his popular book, *Wesen des Christentums* (1900), published in English as *What Is Christianity*, he stated that absolute judgments in history are impossible but that the science of history could reveal the essence of faith. He believed there was no such thing as miracles. In Harnack's version of Christianity, he cleared away the accretions of the early Christian Church. He believed that Christ's very life was his message. According to Harnack, the Christian faith was simple and sublime. "It means one thing and one thing only: Eternal life in the midst of time, by the strength and under the eyes of God."

The German propensity to theological scholarship was matched by a more direct and less abstruse approach to Christianity in the new United States. There, during the Second Great Awakening, Protestant denominations grew rapidly, partly due to the founding of new colleges based on the Christian faith. The pious were encouraged to make personal connections with God. Among the new denominations were the Adventists, which were led by Baptist preacher William Miller (1782-1849). They anticipated the Second Coming of Christ, and when this didn't happen in the period between 1831 and 1844 as predicted by Miller, the Great Disappointment occurred. This was followed by a fracturing of Adventist congregations. The Seventh-day Adventist Church, which was founded from the Millerite movement, distinguished itself by observing Saturday as the Sabbath and promoted fascination with the Second Coming of the Messiah. The Seventh-day Adventist Church established beliefs in the importance of one's diet, adhering to Kosher food laws and advocating vegetarianism.

In the Second Great Awakening, not only was millenarianism, or the Second Coming, emphasized, but there was also a movement among some for a revival in primitive Christianity. The latter was promulgated through missionary camp meetings in which Christian revivalism was promoted, first to the people in the northeast and then westward toward the frontier, where Congregationalist preachers worked to establish not just Christian values but also promoted Christian education.

Among the several sects established during the Second Great Awakening were the Disciples of Christ, also referred to as the Christian Church, and the Church of Jesus Christ of Latter-day Saints, also known as Mormons. The Mormon faith was founded by Joseph Smith (1805-1844), who, thanks to an angel he met in a vision, obtained a book of golden plates inscribed with Judeo-Christian texts concerning the history of American civilization. He translated these and then published them as the *Book of Mormon* (1830). He also founded the Church of Christ (later styled Latter-day Saints). Smith and his followers first moved west to Independence, Missouri, and then Nauvoo, Illinois. Smith was murdered by a mob that was enraged over complaints lodged by dissenting church leaders. His followers moved with a new leader,

Brigham Young (1801-1877), farther west to Salt Lake City in search of a place where they would be free from persecution.

In parts of Europe, the Catholic Church was also subject to the rumblings of reformists. Several men were called from various denominations to preach a new ministry in which they proposed a revival of the original universal church and the perfection of the Christian life. The Catholic Apostolic Church, largely based on the concept of the Second Coming of Christ, disintegrated around the middle of the 19th century. It was replaced by the New Apostolic Church, which, after a number of schisms and theological disputes, flourished in Germany and the Netherlands. The New Apostolic Church was neither wholly Catholic nor Protestant, instead drawing various elements from both.

Throughout the 19th century, the Christian Church was a hotbed of debates on the true meaning of Christ, on forms of worship, and on forms of governance, whether it should be the papacy, the state, or individual congregations. A movement toward the obligation of Christians to engage in social reform developed in the midst of these disputes. A Protestant initiative, the Social Gospel, was particularly favored by the Methodists. It focused on social justice, economic inequality, poverty, and the ills suffered in the working-class slums of major cities. A breakaway denomination was formed by Wesleyan Methodists in 1849. Among their evangelical preachers was William Booth (1829-1912), who believed in the eternal punishment for those who were unbelievers in the gospel of Jesus Christ. He insisted on the necessity of repentance for sin. Booth and his wife established the Christian Revival Society in East London in 1865, focusing his efforts on the poor. He founded God's Army for the propagation of the faith among the disenfranchised, calling it the Salvation Army. The organization of this force for good was based on the military. By the 1880s, Booth's new Christian denomination, the Salvation Army, had expanded to North America and most of the British Empire.

Booth's new Christian army was a part of the Christian renewal in the 19th century, which encompassed what became known as the Social Gospel. Social Gospelers believed that the advent of the Second Coming of Christ could not commence until there was peace and that it was necessary to rid the world of social evils. Social justice, economic equality, and dealing with crime, alcoholism, crime, and racial injustice became rallying points of the Social Gospel. It was particularly strong in the United States, where the Congregationalist preacher Washington Gladden (1836-1918) and the Baptist pastor Walter Rauschenbusch (1861-1918) preached for the return of the ethical principles of Jesus Christ. The Reformists, who followed the lead of these pioneers, established schools, missions, and settlement houses around the United States where the poor and needy could be offered the kind of charity espoused in the message of Jesus Christ. Later in the 20th century, the advocates of the Social Gospel, which included various denominations, came to be associated with the work of labor unions.

While missionaries preaching the Social Gospel fanned out across Great Britain and North America, more traditional missionary activities were sponsored by several denominations. These took the Word of God to the peoples of the world. Among the best known of these 19th-century missionaries was David Livingstone (1813-1873), who was a Congregationalist in the service of the London Missionary Society, which had been formed in 1795 to convert the indigenous peoples of Oceania, Africa, and the Americas to Christianity. Livingstone, who became known to all through the reports of the journalist Henry Morton Stanley (1841-1904), was driven by his faith to travel to Africa, first to Botswana then up to Victoria Falls, where his motto is now inscribed: "Christianity, Commerce and Civilization." Livingstone was as much an explorer and scout for empire-building as he was a missionary in his journeys around Africa.

In America, Protestant missions proved to also be of great significance in propagating the faith. In 1810, the American Board of Commissioners for Foreign Missions (ABCFM) was established as a nondenominational umbrella for missionary work abroad. In its early years, the ABCFM sponsored missionary work among the indigenous peoples of America and vigorously opposed the Indian Removal Act of 1830. By the 1850s, the ABCFM had missions in Africa, western and southern Asia, China, and the North Pacific, as well as missions in the United States to the Choctaws, Cherokees, Dakotas, and several other tribes.

The Social Gospelers' good intentions came to dominate Christian Church activities in the United Kingdom and the United States. Several advocacy organizations were founded. Among them were the Woman's Christian Temperance Union (WCTU), which was established in 1873 in Ohio, USA, and the Elizabeth Fry Society, which was founded in London to advocate for the reform of prisons and the protection of prisoners.

In the 19th century, the Catholic Church was struck by several setbacks, some of which involved purely political matters. In Germany, the chancellor of the newly unified nation, Otto von Bismarck (1815–1898), launched a *Kulturkampf*, or culture war, against the pope and the Catholic Church. At the time, Catholics made up about a third of Germany's population. Bismarck insisted that the Catholic Church and its leader should have no say in the affairs of Germany. Some of the activities in the *Kulturkampf* were unusually draconian. The Pulpit Law (1871) declared that it was illegal for any cleric to discuss issues that displeased the government. Enraged by the harsh measures against them, the German Catholics were instructed by the pope to vote en masse for an anti-Bismarck political party. The issue was resolved with the death of the pope and Bismarck's decision to concentrate on other concerns, such as attacking socialists.

Pope Pius IX (papacy 1848–1878) worked tirelessly to ensure the purity of the Catholic faith and the papal control over all aspects of its ecclesiastical affairs. He called a church council, known as the First Vatican Council, in 1870. The council was called to deal with the increasing dangers of rationalism in theological debates, anarchism, communism, and socialism. In other words, it discussed every form of modern liberal thinking. At the council, the infallibility of the pope was confirmed, but other issues regarding the threats to Roman Catholic theology escaped attention because the council was adjourned. The French troops guarding the Papal States withdrew to deal with the Germans in the Franco-Prussian War. If this were not bad enough for the safety of the pope and his council, those forces working toward the unification of the Italian states occupied Rome. The pope considered himself a prisoner in his own palace. After the council, a number of theologians in Germany were excommunicated on account of their opposition to the concept of papal infallibility.

Chapter 7 – The Church in the 20th and 21st Centuries

The missionary successes at home and abroad of various Protestant sects in the 19th century brought fervent evangelicals into the fold, who themselves worked to convert not only non-Christians but also Catholics. At the same time, in Europe, vast swaths of the unfortunate poor were left to wallow in the shades of smoke-belching factories. This environment forced the Catholic Church to directly confront the pressures of the modern age. The impact of public discourse on such new subjects as secularism and the rise of discussion of such words as "agnostic" and "atheist" was such that urgent action was required of the Roman Catholic Church to deal with modernism and its role in the Catholic faith. Pope Pius X (papacy 1903–1914) led the Roman Catholic Church in its battle against heretical modernism by issuing an encyclical *Pascendi Dominici gregis*, or, in English, *Feeding the Lord's Flock* (1907). Through the encyclical, the pope officially condemned some of the tenets of modernism as heresy. It was notions of God, man's position in the world, and his life in the now and the hereafter, which had been originally proposed by humanist scholars, that irked the Catholic Church. The kind of writing that was particularly threatening to the orthodox faith was primarily from the pens of Protestants. An example of a work that the Catholics condemned was Paul Sabatier's (1858-1928) *Life of Francis of Assisi* (1893), which was placed on the Catholic Index of Forbidden Books because it took issue with the canonical story of the medieval saint.

The kind of thinking that Pius X wanted to counter can be exemplified by the work of Louis Auguste Sabatier (1839-1901). Sabatier was a Protestant professor in Paris who advanced the cause of liberalism. His inquiry was centered on how the Christian faith might adjust to "modernity." He noted traditional theology was based on authority, but in the modern world, it was gradually being replaced by autonomous reason and the experimental method. "If theology persists in subjecting itself to an ancient method from which all other disciplines have freed themselves, it will not only find itself in sterile isolation, but it will expose itself to the irrefutable denials and unchallengeable judgments of a reason always more and more independent and certain of itself."

Modernism was, in fact, a somewhat disconnected series of propositions that traditionalists in the Catholic Church were disinclined to attack one by one. A blanket condemnation of modernism was that it was a simple method to deal with complex ideas. One such modern idea was historicism or historism. It posited that all human institutions, including religion, are subject to constant change. Historicists denied that things changed in relation to an end goal or purpose, which was distinctly un-Christian. The historicist philosophical propositions that objective truth is received subjectively and that the true subject of religion was man were considered heretical. The fact that proponents of the Social Gospel were becoming actors on the political stage and the fact that their activism was not controlled by an ecclesiastical hierarchy alarmed the Catholic Church. In post-revolutionary France, a movement among the Catholic clergy, called Liberal Catholicism, was an attempt to reconcile the church with liberal democracy. It was expanded to include an effort to mediate the differences between the Catholic faith and modern society and science. According to Pius X, this was yet another example in which scholar/ecclesiastics could fall into error.

The condemnation of modernism, called a "synthesis of all heresies" by Pope Pius X, was a broad net to encompass a variety of thinking in the modern world. In order to ensure success in stamping out all the embers of modernist thought in the Catholic Church, an anti-modernist oath was required of all clergymen. This included all those brothers and sisters in orders dedicated to the education of youth. As different regions often followed laws differently, Pope Pius X clarified the matter by instituting the first universal Code of Canon Law in 1917. Canon law regulated the organization, government, and order of the church and set out rules governing human behavior as Catholics pursued the church's mission.

A significant Christian sect that arose in the mid-20th century evolved from Zion's Watch Tower Tract Society, which was one strand of the Bible Student movement in America in the late 19th century. In 1931, the Watch Tower Tract Society became the Jehovah's Witnesses. Jehovah's Witnesses held that the Second Coming was the goal of society. They did not believe in the Holy Trinity, the inherent immortality of the soul, or the existence of hell and were pacifists. Christian holidays and customs, like birthdays, were pagan in origin and thus incompatible with Christianity.

Pentecostalism began in the early 20th century in the United States. At the time, those preachers, who developed doctrines based on what they called the baptism with the Holy Spirit, usually separated themselves from their church. However, toward the middle of the century, Pentecostals became accepted into the mainline denominations as they became associated with high-powered Christian revivals led by preachers like the very popular

Billy Graham (1918-2018) and mass healings by charismatic pastors such as Oral Roberts (1918-2009).

To some extent, the rise of charismatic Pentecostal and evangelical churches in America and abroad in the 20th century can be seen as a movement to counter the worldwide threat of communism, which was, according to the new fervent religious, "Godless," as the Soviet Union and the People's Republic of China established state atheism. One of the most spectacular periods of growth of evangelicalism in the 20th century was in Central America, where various states were threatened with the rise of communist insurgents. It appeared at one point that the sway of the Catholic Church in the region was in peril. The Catholic Church was quite frequently painted as being in the hands of conservative dictators. It also seemed as if its regional authorities were blind to the suffering of the *campesinos* and indigenous peoples under autocratic governments. This was not entirely true, although some clerics did condone repressive governments.

Some clerics in Central America believed the Social Gospel applied to their faith. Óscar Romero, who was the leader of the Catholic Church in El Salvador, spoke out against the government's abuses of power and condemned assassinations, torture, poverty, and social injustice. He was assassinated in 1980 while celebrating Mass. A truth commission was established to look into the murder, and it concluded that a right-wing politician named Roberto D'Aubuisson, who was backed by the United States, had given the order to kill the archbishop of San Salvador.

The circumstances under which Archbishop Romero fell afoul of the right-wing in El Salvador can be traced back to the Second Vatican Council (1962-1965). It was called to define the position of the Catholic Church in the modern world. Many of the changes that took place were to engage the faithful more fully. Vernacular languages replaced Latin in the celebration of Mass. The priests officiating at Mass were now permitted to face the congregation.

Church music was modernized, prayers were revised, and the church calendar was abbreviated, eliminating many saint's days. The Second Vatican Council, which was presided over by Pope John XXIII (papacy 1958-1963), considered a vast number of issues, including restoring unity among all Christians, the recognition of the legitimacy of the Eastern Catholic Churches (Eastern Orthodox Churches), and the reverent attitude of Catholics to non-Christian religions.

With the way open for more liberal notions within the Catholic Church, certain theologians in Latin America explored ecclesiastical "concern for the poor and political liberation for oppressed peoples." It became accepted by several Latin American clerics that they were to serve as advocates for liberation theology. This new theology stood at the nexus of Christian theology and political activism. It involved seeing theology from the point of view of the poor and the oppressed. The growth of this activist theology was spectacular, for the indigenous peoples and the poor looked to their local parish priests to lead them from their hopeless conditions. It was this kind of Social Gospel, or God's words in action, that led to the assassination of Archbishop Romero.

On the opposite side of theological thinking in the Catholic Church were monks who had continued in the tradition of their medieval forebears. Arguably the most influential of these monks in the 20th century was the Trappist Thomas Merton (1915-1968). The Trappists are officially known as the Order of Cistercians of the Strict Observance. Thomas Merton was a resident of the Abbey of Our Lady of Gethsemani in Kentucky, USA, and over his lifetime of contemplation and thought, he found time to write more than fifty books. The most popular of them was his autobiography, *The Seven Storey Mountain* (1948). It inspired many returning American veterans from WWII to consider dedicating themselves to Christ by retiring in monasteries.

The mystical aspect of Merton's theology fit nicely with the West's interest in Eastern religion after the publication of William James's *The Varieties of Religious Experience: A Study in Human Nature*, a series of lectures given in 1901 and 1902. Throughout the 20th century, perhaps in response to the horrors of two catastrophic world wars, the idea that Christian theology could be fused with mysticism gained a currency that it had not had since the Late Middle Ages. In the midst of the First World War, Christian mysticism in England had a strong following. Among these enthusiasts was the poet Arthur Edward Waite (1857–1942), who was an occultist steeped in esoteric religion. His Fellowship of the Rosy Cross, which was modeled after medieval knightly orders such as the Templars, attracted several like-minded mystics, among whom was British novelist Charles Williams (1886–1945).

The long-established denominations of the Christian Church all encountered problems with respect to the swift changes in society that occurred in the 20th century. In many countries where Catholicism had been strong, the number of congregants dropped off precipitously. Conflicts with the secular state—first over divorce, then over birth control, and finally over abortion—resulted in a drop-off in the number of professed Catholics. The same occurred in jurisdictions where the state, in response to changes in social mores, actively sought convictions of ecclesiastics for sex crimes stretching back many years. These crimes often were covered up by church authorities, who now find their positions in jeopardy. Further, diocesan assets have been seized to pay for damages. This has meant a diminution of Catholic Church property such as never before seen in the entire history of the church. As if this were not enough, the Catholic Church has, since the late 20th century, faced increasing pressure to accept the equality of women and men in the church bureaucracy and in the celebration of Mass. Seven Catholic women (the Danube Seven) from various countries were ordained as priests aboard a cruise ship in 2002. They were accused of violating canon law, which states that only males can be ordained priests. They were threatened with and subsequently excommunicated. Since then, women priests have been automatically excommunicated by the pope. The Catholic Church cannot tolerate the ordination of women because, as Pope John Paul II (papacy 1978-2005) wrote, "The Church has no authority whatsoever to confer priestly ordination of women and... this judgment is to be definitively held by all the Church's faithful."

The Anglican Church (the Episcopalian Church in the USA) has managed the transition from male domination to gender equality much more nimbly than the Catholic Church. This is in part due to the organization of the church's hierarchy. In some of the more progressive Anglican dioceses, women have been ordained priests since the 1970s. Since celibacy is not a requirement for the Anglican priesthood, the number of women seeking to enter the profession or calling to serve God as a priest is much more than those wishing to become priests in the Catholic faith. The first female bishop in the Anglican, or Episcopalian, Church was installed in the USA in 1989. Since then, female bishops have been appointed in about a dozen dioceses.

The most surprising of all the changes in the Christian Church in the 20th and 21st centuries is the rise of evangelical Pentecostal churches around the world. The Pentecostal World Fellowship, which was founded in 1947, acts as an umbrella organization for some 279 million Pentecostals in over 700 denominations. The Pentecostal statement of faith includes, "We believe in the ministry of the Holy Spirit by whose indwelling the Christian is enabled to live a Godly life." This statement hints at how the Pentecostal movement has become allied with the charismatic Christian movement, whose theology emphasizes the work of the Holy Spirit, spiritual gifts, and miracles as part of a believer's everyday life. Pentecostal and charismatic Christians together number over 584 million people worldwide, comprising more than a quarter of the two billion Christians in the world.

At the present day, in the richest countries in the world, Christian congregations are rapidly declining. This is primarily a phenomenon in the Catholic Church and some Protestant denominations. However, in the less wealthy regions of the world, church membership is expanding rapidly. What this has meant to the Christian Church is that the center of theological training and the location of some of the most radical thinking in the church is now not in Europe or North America. The shifting control over affairs in the Catholic Church is evidenced by the appointment of the Argentinian Jorge Mario Bergoglio as Pope Francis in 2013. He is the first non-European to fill this role. The same kind of shift is occurring in the Anglican Church. John Tucker Mugabi Sentamu, a native of Uganda and a refugee in England, served as the archbishop of York and the primate of England from 2005 to 2020. If nothing else, the election of Pope Francis and Archbishop Sentamu suggest that the Christian Church as an institution is in flux. But change occurs at different rates among the various denominations. More than a few of these have prohibitions against divorce, abortion, and same-sex marriage. Some prohibit gays and lesbians from holding church offices. This will doubtless change when these kinds of prohibitions are not followed by the secular state.

Conclusion

It is risky at best to predict the future of the Christian Church. As an institution in the social fabric of a community or nation, it has survived incredible challenges by contending theologians, battling clerics, conflicts between emperors, kings, and popes, disputes over laws and ethics, and fights over the historical veracity of almost every event and meaning of practically every word in the Bible. The Christian Church has split and split again, which has led to thousands of denominations of Christians spread around the globe. All disagree on some point or another on how a Christian should live their life. What they do have in common is little more than the acceptance of Jesus Christ standing at the core of their faith. They differ over who he was, what he did, what he said, and what happened when he died. The churches also differ on who should or could lead the congregants, whether it be chaste males, females and males, only those filled with the spirit of the Holy Ghost, only heterosexuals, and so on. Differences are what have made the Christian Church so vital and exceptional in the history of the world.

The dominance of the Christian Church in many states in the Western world has lately been challenged by the incursion of non-Christian religions that have been transported across borders by global immigration. Frictions between Christians and non-Christians are clothed in cultural or ethnic differences that become entrenched as economic discrimination. Thus, it is often difficult to disentangle religious differences from racial and cultural differences. One of the most significant challenges faced by the Christian Church in the West is how to incorporate all aspects of liberalism into a faith that is historically based on the concept that it is the one and only true faith. Some have even gone so far as to call for a new Christian crusade to deal with the perceived danger of encroaching non-Christian religions, in particular, the global resurgence of Islam. Wars fought under the guise of religion, whether they are between Catholics and Protestants, as in Northern Ireland in the time of the Troubles (1960s to 1990s), or between Christians and Muslims, will pose particular problems for liberal-leaning members of the Christian Church.

The single most important aspect of the Christian Church's evolution as an institution in society is that it is always in a state of dynamic change. Changes in theology, in concepts of divinity, and in the organization of churches of all stripes are built into the very fabric of Christianity itself. The Christian Church, in general, has the capacity to look backward, deal with the status quo, and then look forward. Many Christians see this capacity as an essential part of the message of Jesus Christ.

Part 2: The Reformation

A Captivating Guide to the Religious Revolution Sparked by Martin Luther and Its Impact on Christianity and the Western Church

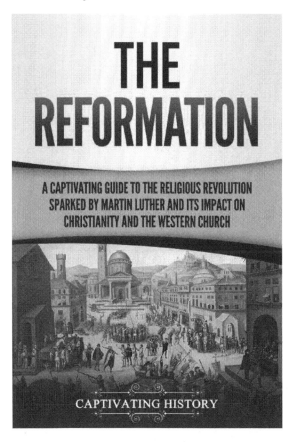

THE
REFORMATION

A CAPTIVATING GUIDE TO THE RELIGIOUS REVOLUTION
SPARKED BY MARTIN LUTHER AND ITS IMPACT ON
CHRISTIANITY AND THE WESTERN CHURCH

CAPTIVATING HISTORY

Introduction: How the Reformation was Unleashed

In the early 1500s, Christianity was about as united as it would ever be. During this period, there were only two main branches of Christianity: the Catholicism of the West and the Orthodox Church of the East. East and West had split some 500 years prior due to some rather minor (yet consequential) doctrinal differences. It was only when the external threat of the advancing armies of Islam began the first of many attempts to batter down the doors of the Eastern Orthodox Church—whose seat was in Constantinople (modern-day Istanbul)—that the Catholic Church and the Orthodox Church attempted to mend fences.

Christendom launched Crusades from the West in an attempt to defend its eastern brothers, but in the end, the Eastern Orthodox Church, once headquartered in Asia Minor (modern-day Turkey), was overrun and subjugated to Islam. The remnants of Orthodox Christianity would survive, but in its tattered form, it would no longer pose a significant challenge to the Catholic Church as far as ideology. It wasn't until a man named Martin Luther began to question Catholic teachings in the early 1500s that new fractures in the church structure became visible.

Martin Luther became a Catholic priest in 1507. He was a dedicated member of the clergy but began to have serious misgivings with many aspects of official Catholic doctrine. The questions that began to arise in the heart of this lone monk led to him famously nailing his Ninety-five Theses to the doors of All Saints' Church (sometimes referred to as Castle Church) where he served. On October 31, 1517, about a decade after Luther's original ordination, he nailed his chief protests to the church doors for all to see.

The modern reader will note the date since it has since become associated with Halloween. Back in Luther's day, it was known as All Saints' Eve since the following day was November 1, which was (and still is) the Catholic holiday of All Saints' Day. All Saints' Day was also called All Hallows' Day in various quarters, and the night before would have been known as All Hallows' Eve, from which we get the modern variation of Halloween.

But as spooky as all that might sound, Luther, it seems, chose this date for no other reason than the fact that All Saints' Day (All Hallows' Day) was when many budding intellectuals of the church would meet. Knowing many people would be there on that day to discuss his treatises, he posted them on the door the day before so everyone would be sure to see them. The posting of these directives was not that unusual, either.

Many have likened his posting on the doors to someone posting notes on a bulletin board (or better yet, on Facebook) just to air an opinion. Martin Luther wasn't trying to do anything all that radical at the time—he was simply opening a dialogue and asking a few questions. Luther never intended to break up the Catholic Church or create opposing factions; he just sought to reform (hence the phrase Reformation) the Catholic Church from within. But little did he know the tidal wave of change he was about to unleash.

Chapter 1 – Martin's Ninety-Five Reasons for Reform

"From the beginning of my Reformation I have asked God to send me neither dreams, nor visions, nor angels, but to give me the right understanding of his Word, and the Holy Scriptures. For as long as I have God's Word, I know that I am walking in His way and that I shall not fall into any error or delusion."

Martin Luther

Much has been made of the Ninety-five Theses (or theological propositions) that Martin Luther nailed up on the abbey door in 1517. But what did they entail? Despite the extraordinary social change they would spark, the theses themselves were not exactly radical in nature, and they focused on two main themes: Luther's belief that salvation was achieved by faith rather than works and Luther's insistence that Scripture should be the ultimate religious authority rather than clergy.

Of chief concern to Luther at the time was the fact that the church had been in the business of selling salvation to the masses through something called an indulgence. This practice allowed parishioners to literally give money to the Catholic Church in exchange for promises from the clergy to forgive them of sin and/or grant them passage from purgatory to Heaven. To understand the practice of indulgences, one must understand the teachings of the Catholic Church of this time period.

Catholics taught that sinners needed to undergo penance in this life and—often enough—also in the next. It was a common belief of the time that upon passing, most people didn't go immediately to Heaven or hell but rather to an in-between realm called purgatory. Since Luther's day, many Protestant groups have thoroughly ridiculed the idea of purgatory and have even gone so far as to say the Catholic Church made the whole thing up.

But although the word purgatory—a Latin word meaning to cleanse or purge—is most definitely not in Scripture, there is biblical mention of just such a place. The Bible did indeed often speak of an in-between or limbo realm where the saints "sleep." This place has been referred to by its Hebrew name of Sheol. The original Greek of the New Testament used the Greek word for Sheol, which is Hades, to describe the same exact place. The same realm has also come through translation as "paradise," or even "Abraham's Bosom."

It can be confusing to have such pleasant-sounding names as "paradise" and "Abraham's Bosom" for a place Catholic's called purgatory. Also of confusion is the use of the Greek word "Hades," which most people probably associate with the Western concept of hell, but hell and Hades are two different concepts. While hell is defined as a place of torment, Hades is simply the underworld abode of the dead.

The actual Greek term for a place of torment akin to our common notion of hell is the word "Tartarus." In the Greek translation of the New Testament, the word "Tartarus" only appears one time when the Apostle Peter is describing the final destination of the fallen angels who disobeyed God. The choice of this word is interesting because, in Greek mythology, Tartarus is the place where the Titans were imprisoned. If you read up on Greek myths and compare them with the biblical stories of the fallen angels/watchers/Nephilim, the parallels are rather stunning.

It makes one wonder, was the word "Tartarus" chosen out of convenience, or was it indeed referring to the same exact place? Did the Apostle Peter see some sort of similarity between the popular Greek tales of the Titans and the fallen angels? At any rate, as it pertains to Sheol, Hades, paradise, and Abraham's Bosom—all these realms spoken of in the Bible, regardless of what they are called, fulfill the same purpose of the Catholic purgatory. They are neither Heaven nor hell, but merely a place where transitory souls are temporarily holed up.

These concepts are complex, and save for theologians who spend years studying them in- depth, most Christians probably do not know much about them. But, as strange as they may sound to the casual observer, these concepts are based on Scripture. Early Christians believed that before Jesus came to Earth and died on the cross, all the Old Testament saints (such as Abraham) were denied access to Heaven, yet God certainly wasn't going to send them to hell, so instead, they were kept in an in-between plane of existence—hence Abraham's bosom, paradise, purgatory, Sheol, or whatever you wish to call it.

According to this notion, Jesus himself, after being crucified, descended down into this netherworld to "set the captives free." Today, preachers are more likely to use this as an allegory to deliver a feel-good message to the masses about how Jesus liberates those in bondage to things such as alcohol or some other vice. There is certainly nothing wrong with that, but the expression has a literal interpretation, as well. The three days between Christ's crucifixion and resurrection is a dramatic part of New Testament Scripture that is often overlooked, but according to the Bible, he wasn't idle.

Scripture tells us that immediately after being killed on the cross, Jesus went straight to paradise/purgatory and quite literally "led captivity captive" by rescuing the Old Testament saints who were being held in Sheol. It was only after this mission was complete that Jesus Christ was physically resurrected from the dead and emerged from the tomb—back from the dead and back from that underworld realm of purgatory called Sheol/Hades.

According to the Bible, in the three days prior to his resurrection, Jesus was on a spiritual mission to set souls who had long been stuck in a purgatory limbo free. He did not enter Heaven until his physical resurrection and eventual ascension in what Christians refer to as his "glorified" or "immortal/incorruptible" body—a state of being that Christians believe they, too, will be transformed into in the "twinkling of an eye" when the "last trumpet sounds."

The idea that Jesus went to paradise first, before resurrection and ascension, is also supported by a remark Jesus made to the thief on the cross: "This day you will be with me in paradise." He didn't say Heaven but specifically said "paradise," which is another word for Sheol/Abraham's Bosom/Hades—you get the point.

This is a lot to unpack, but understanding such things is essential to understanding why Catholics spoke of an in-between realm called purgatory. Despite misinformation and the insinuation that purgatory is simply nonsense someone made up, the concept of purgatory is one that is grounded in Scripture.

At any rate, Catholics greatly expanded upon all of this and eventually came to believe that one could lessen the time spent in purgatory by paying indulgences to priests—or even help dead relatives believed to be in purgatory by paying on their behalf. As for Martin Luther, it is said that he would later drop much of his previous belief in purgatory, but at the time he nailed his Ninety-five Theses to the door, he wasn't so much against the notion of purgatory itself as the idea that one could pay their way out of it.

As corrupt as such a bargain might seem at first glance, the act of paying money or "alms" on behalf of a deceased loved one wasn't simply a scheme hatched by the Catholic Church. Just like purgatory, it was derived from Scripture. The concept of indulgences stems from Maccabees—a book which, coincidentally enough, is excluded from most Protestant Bibles. The concept of paying a sacrificial amount of money for the souls of the departed comes from an account of Judas Maccabeus advising his followers to pay alms for some of his warriors who had perished in battle.

These warriors were found to have amulets around their necks that were considered profane and in reverence to pagan gods. It was for the atonement of the acts of these dead men that Judas requested all his followers to offer up alms. Or, as 2 Maccabees 42-45 tells us, "The noble Judas called on the people to keep themselves free from sin, for they had seen with their own eyes what had happened to the fallen because of their sin. He levied a contribution from each man and sent the total of two thousand silver drachmas to Jerusalem for a sin offering—a fit and proper act in which he took due account of the resurrection. For if he had not been expecting the fallen to rise again, it would have been foolish and superfluous to pray for the dead. But since he had in view the wonderful reward reserved for those who die a godly death, his purpose was a holy and pious one. And this was why he offered an atoning sacrifice to free the dead from their sin."

Maccabees clearly gives an example of praying for the dead and paying alms (an indulgence) for them in the hopes that this atoning sacrifice would "free the dead from their sin." Protestant Bibles would choose not to include the Book of Maccabees. Roman Catholic priests however, could readily point to this one Scripture as part of their reasoning behind allowing indulgences to be made for those offering alms for the dearly departed.

As it pertains to Martin Luther's reasons for nailing his Ninety-five Theses to the church doors on October 31, 1517, he was primarily critical of what he saw as blatant abuses of the practice. Luther was particularly irked by priests who had used the sales of indulgences to fund building projects. In Luther's day, the acquisition of indulgences had become so thoroughly commercialized that, at one point, a Dominican friar by the name of Johan Tetzel had created his own advertising jingle to get proceeds. The crafty friar was allegedly fond of proclaiming, "As soon as the coin in the coffer rings, a soul from purgatory to heaven springs!"

Luther believed that such malfeasance was corrupting to the clergy just as much as it was to the congregation since it made the public think they could avoid true repentance and simply pay their way into Heaven instead. Martin Luther decisively condemned such practices in Thesis 32 of his Ninety-five Theses, which stated, "Those who believe that they can be certain of their salvation because they have indulgence letters will be eternally damned, together with their teachers." In Thesis 43, he then further clarified this belief when he declared, "Christians are to be taught that he who gives to the poor or lends to the needy does a better deed than he who buys indulgences."

He also decisively rebuked the Church's practice of using indulgence money to fund building projects. In Thesis 50, Luther had steadfastly proclaimed, "Christians are to be taught that if the pope knew the exactions of the indulgence preachers, he would rather that the basilica of St. Peter were burned to ashes than built up with the skin, flesh, and bones of his sheep."

It's important to note that while Luther excoriated clergy, whom he called "indulgence preachers," he still managed to hold the pope himself blameless. When Luther nailed his Ninety-five Theses to those church doors, he still believed that the pope was not aware of what lower-level clergy (most especially the likes of Johan Tetzel) were doing.

Instead, Martin Luther insisted that the pope was ignorant of such things, and if he only knew, "he would rather that the basilica of St. Peter were burned to ashes than built up with the skin, flesh, and bones of his sheep." As you can see, at this point in his own personal evolution of thought, Luther was willing to give the pope in faraway Rome the benefit of the doubt—his views, however, would soon change.

Chapter 2 – Luther Gets Labeled a Heretic

"Unless I am convicted by Scripture and plain reason, I do not accept the authority of popes and councils, for they have contradicted each other. My conscience is captive to the Word of God. I cannot and will not recant anything, for to go against conscience is neither right nor safe. Here I stand, I cannot do otherwise. God help me. Amen."

Martin Luther

In the immediate aftermath of Martin Luther nailing his Ninety-five Theses to the doors of Wittenberg's Castle Church, his religious tracts made the rounds and were circulated freely. Luther's words seemed to resonate with the German masses, who were largely disenchanted with Rome's grip over local church affairs. Luther's daring rebukes stirred up their own skepticism of papal authority. But, by the time copies of Luther's theses reached Rome itself, the reaction was initially one of indifference.

Roman clergy believed that Luther's main argument was against the Dominican order of friars such as Johan Tetzel, an order that was often at odds with the Augustinian order to which Martin Luther belonged. Luther did indeed criticize Tetzel and seemed to shield the pope himself from blame, merely pointing out the perceived abuses of the clergy under his authority. Luther, in fact, had professed his belief that if the pope only knew of the abuses that were occurring, he was certain to put a stop to it.

Martin Luther presented himself as a faithful priest who had a disagreement with how other priests conducted themselves, so it's understandable why Roman Catholic authorities initially shrugged off the whole thing as a petty squabble between monks. Yet, as the debate continued to rage and more voices became involved in the drama, the Vatican couldn't help but take notice.

By 1518, Luther's words were being printed in both Latin and German, and although he never gained a copyright or royalties from his work, his tracts had become something of a best seller. Soon, everyone was talking about the ideas of this previously unknown and obscure Augustinian monk. It was while riding this wave of interest that Luther made his way to the University of Heidelberg in April of 1518 to speak freely to a live audience.

Even at this point, there was concern over Luther's personal security since some people had already shown strong opposition to his teachings. Nevertheless, the local German authority—the Elector of Saxony, Frederick the Wise—granted Luther a letter guaranteeing safe passage should anyone try to intercept him. In the meantime, Luther did not have the intention of stirring up debate during this visit. His original plans were to deliver a lecture over the merits of Saint Augustine's theology. As an Augustinian monk himself, this was certainly some well-trod territory.

Yet, for those who had gathered, the main draw was not to hear about St. Augustine, but rather the growing controversy over Luther's Ninety-five Theses. They especially wanted to hear Luther reference his recent arguments against the practice of indulgences. And, while Luther did not delve too deeply into his ideas on indulgences, he did touch on other matters that would be extremely important to the coming Reformation. He spoke of his views on the righteousness of faith through Christ and expounded on his notion of the utter impotence of human beings to achieve their own salvation.

Luther's lecture at Heidelberg was well received and a great success, rendering him almost a local celebrity. But as his fame grew, so did his opposition. By the summer of 1518, he was being assailed by one of the top Catholic minds in the region—John Eck. Eck took direct issue with Luther's Ninety-five Theses and wrote his own opposition piece, titled "Obelisks." Here, Eck railed against Luther and attempted to tear apart his arguments.

Luther was initially stunned by the onslaught, never imagining that someone like Eck could take such an issue with his mere questioning of a practice such as indulgences. Luther soon got over his shock, however, and went on the offensive. Holding nothing back, he picked up his pen and unleashed upon his opponent in the bombastic manner that would make him famous. At one point, he famously declared Eck to be behaving like nothing more than "an irritated prostitute" that vomits up terrible curses and oaths.

With rhetoric like this, there was no going back. A line had been drawn in the sand, and as it pertained to Luther, either you loved the man or you thought he was an abominable heretic. Soon enough, even faraway Rome was setting things in motion to silence this troublesome monk. On August 7, 1518, Luther was stunned to receive official correspondence from the Vatican, which proclaimed that his Ninety-five Theses were deemed heretical. As such, Luther was asked to report to Rome to answer for his errors.

This was a dangerous prospect for Luther, however, since it meant he would have to leave his relatively safe German backyard and present himself in Rome at the complete mercy of the Vatican— an institution which, in those days, was usually not too kind to those whom it believed to be leading the flock astray. As it were, in fact, there were already a few schemes afoot to forcibly arrest Luther. If possible, the German Augustinians were instructed to lay hold of Luther and "send him to Rome bound hand and foot in chains."

A sign of the weakening hold of Rome was apparent, however, in the fact that this never occurred. During Luther's day, the so-called "Holy Roman Empire" was the real powerhouse. And, although the spiritual center of the Holy Roman Empire was meant to be in Rome, the political center of the Holy Roman Empire of Luther's time was in the German principalities of Central Europe. (To clear up any confusion, it's important to note that "Germany" as we know it today had yet to be born. Sure, there were Germanic peoples who spoke German, of which Martin Luther himself was a part, but the modern nation-state of Germany would not come about until 1871.) During Luther's day, what we now call Germany was a part of the Holy Roman Empire, which at that time encompassed what is now modern-day Germany, Austria, Switzerland, part of France, part of Italy, and part of Poland. Accordingly, instead of being sent to Rome, Luther was instead given the option of going to the imperial parliament of the German city of Augsburg in October of 1518.

Here Luther was personally questioned by the papal legate of Augsburg, a fellow by the name of Cardinal Cajetan, over the course of three days. It was Cardinal Cajetan who repeatedly insisted that Luther was wrong and demanded that he correct his "errors" over the practice of indulgences and his views on the extent of papal authority. Luther refused, however, and shortly thereafter, Cardinal Cajetan labeled Luther a heretic, and requested the German authorities either "send him to Rome or chase him from Saxony."

Luther himself knew that his freedom was very much in jeopardy at this point, and as such, quickly left Augsburg for safer ground in northern Germany. Again, it is important to consider the political situation in the region at that time. The land we more commonly call Germany, was a part of the Holy Roman Empire. In 1518, this empire was ruled by the Holy Roman Emperor, Maximilian I. As fate would have it, Maximilian abruptly passed away in January of 1519. This left his grandson, Charles V, as his successor.

Charles could not become the official ruler of the HRE (Holy Roman Empire) until he was chosen by the seven imperial electors—yes, interestingly, the Holy Roman Emperor was ultimately chosen by an "electoral college." In much the same manner as a United States president is chosen by electors scattered throughout fifty states, the Holy Roman Emperor was put in power by the seven electors of the HRE, who were also in charge of various principalities in the region.

The electors would designate the next monarchical candidate as the emperor-elect before final confirmation was given by the pope. All this might indeed sound almost amusing to an American reader due to its similarities to the United States electoral college, electors, and the concept of having a president-elect until the new leader is officially confirmed. But, as it turns out, the Founding Fathers of America borrowed many of their ideas from other places and times; the concept of the electoral college was one such notion they grafted into the US constitution.

At any rate, the electors represented important territories such as Cologne, Mainz, Trier, Saxony, Palatine of the Rhine, Margrave of Brandenburg, and Bohemia. These regions made up what was known as the "Imperial Diet," which was considered a deliberative body of the Holy Roman Empire. It was in this deliberative forum that much of Luther's later debates would take place.

At the time of Maximilian's death, Luther was living under the jurisdiction of the Elector of Saxony, the German Prince Frederick III. Frederick was a conservative when it came to religion, but he also happened to be the founder of Wittenberg and a stalwart champion of its resident theologian—Martin Luther. Luther had a great protector in the form of Frederick III, and as such, Rome had to tread cautiously when dealing with him. They could call him a heretic, but lest the pope alienate one of the electors of the HRE, Rome could not directly intervene.

Chapter 3 – Martin Luther Gets Ready for Battle

"The world doesn't want to be punished. It wants to remain in darkness. It doesn't want to be told that what it believes is false. If you also don't want to be corrected, then you might as well leave the church and spend your time at the bar and brothel. But if you want to be saved and remember that there's another life after this one you must accept correction."

Martin Luther

Either divine providence or just plain old good luck created some rather fortuitous circumstances for Martin Luther in 1519. It was that year that Holy Roman Emperor Maximillian perished, and the contest began for a new emperor to be declared by the HRE's electoral college. In the meantime, the mini-ruler of the place Luther resided—the Elector of Saxony, Prince Frederick III—was a man who was determined to keep the realm under his control and entirely free from Roman interference.

The University of Wittenberg in which Luther taught was also a site of extreme importance for the region, and Luther was a valuable member of the faculty. As such, Frederick III was not about to allow power players in Rome to simply snatch Luther up and take him away. Instead, Frederick remained adamant that Luther, as a German theologian, needed to be tried by a German court.

Pope Leo X, on the other hand, was not willing to press his luck on the matter since he was dependent upon Elector Frederick when it came to the electoral vote. Luther, in the meantime, was dependent on this valuable elector's protection. It was with this assurance that he continued to debate Catholic clergy.

One of the most famous of these debates took place in June of 1519 when Luther made his way to Leipzig to face off with Johann Eck, a faithful member of the Roman Catholic Church. Eck was considered an intelligent and esteemed theologian among his peers, but Luther referred to him as nothing more than a "little glory-hungry beast." In his debate with Eck, Luther stressed that Christian doctrine should not be directed by the supposed infallibility of the pope, but rather the Bible, or as Luther put it, "the infallible word of God."

Eck was rather belligerent in his attempts to rebuff Luther's assertions but dogmatically insisted that it was heresy to question allegiance to the pope. Luther, however, was quick to point out that the early church (as in the days of the apostles and shortly thereafter) had no papal authority to follow, and the Greek Orthodox Church, which had parted ways with the Catholic Church since the Great Schism, was no longer following directives from the pope, either. Luther used these two precedents to bolster his claim that the pope should not be the beat-all, end-all authority in matters of faith.

Luther had not yet officially broken with the pope; he was just stressing the need to be able to question papal directives. Even so, in more private communications, Luther had gone so far as to openly speculate that perhaps the pope was "the Antichrist himself." Luther was not quite prepared for the masterful performance that seasoned debater Johann Eck put on. Luther's delivery was rushed, and he is said to have seemed agitated and even a little unhinged throughout the engagement.

The audience also didn't seem too pleased when Luther began to suggest that purgatory might not be scriptural after all—even though theologians like Eck were more than ready to point to specific Scriptures to bolster their interpretation. But the moment that Eck truly let loose on Luther was when he mentioned John Huss, a reformer that lived some 100 years prior and was burned at the stake for his beliefs. Eck was probably bringing up Huss to frighten Luther and remind him of what might possibly be in store for him if he persisted.

Luther refused to back down, however, and remarked that Huss very well could have been right in some of his assertions. One can imagine the gasp let out by those in attendance. This was the trap that Eck had laid for Luther, and he didn't hesitate to take advantage of it. As soon as he had Luther identifying with a confirmed heretic, it was easy for Eck to paint Luther as one and the same.

It was soon after his engagement with Johann Eck that the local universities began to move against Luther, with many of them burning his writings and making pronouncements against him. But Martin Luther proved himself to be just as shrewd of a politician as he was a theologian. While the clergy were being encouraged to condemn Luther, he was contacting all the major political players in the region and stoking their sense of nationalism, in opposition to what was perceived as foreign interference.

Yes, as much as Martin Luther was a religious reformer, in many ways, he was also a German nationalist who decried foreign interference from Rome. As such, he didn't hesitate to play upon the German authorities' independent streak in encouraging them to aid him in his reformation of the church. He informed them that the Bible calls all Christians to act and made it clear that they did not need to wait for papal directives from Rome to do so.

As one might imagine, the Catholic Church would not take such things kindly. By the following summer of 1520, the pope issued a papal bull (official edict) in which the philosophies of Martin Luther were labeled a "poisonous virus." The pope highlighted what he perceived to be forty different errors in Martin Luther's ideology and gave Luther sixty days to present himself to the Vatican to answer to these supposed errors or risk being excommunicated from the church.

Martin Luther was not shaken or in any way deterred, however. Sixty days later, rather than report to Rome, Luther and his followers lit a bonfire in which they burned Roman Catholic literature—including the very papal bull that had been sent to him. As Luther cast the papal bull into the fire, he is said to have declared, regarding the pope, "Because you have confounded the truth of God, today the Lord confounds you. Into the fire with you!"

The pope finally answered this challenge by issuing another papal bull on January 3, 1521, which officially excommunicated Martin Luther, as well as those who followed him. He was accused of having a depraved mind and of being the leader of a "pernicious and heretical sect." In the past, such a condemnation would have brought those guilty of the trespasses to Rome to face punishment, but Luther continued to be protected by the local ruler, Frederick III.

Instead of being extradited to Rome, Luther was asked to show up at the next scheduled meeting of the Imperial Diet, which was set to take place in a town called Worms. This gathering would be presided over by the newly-elected Holy Roman Emperor, Charles V. This guaranteed Luther safe passage to the forum, but there was still the risk that he would be clandestinely seized by forces working for the Vatican and hauled off to face the pope.

Martin Luther himself knew full well the risk he was taking by going to the Diet of Worms, but he decided that he had to hold firm regardless. He voiced his sentiment to a close confidant of his at the time by stating, "If God does not want to preserve me, then my head is of slight importance compared with Christ." Luther figured that if God wished for him and his work to continue, his safety would be assured. If not, then it would not be of much importance in the long run. Arming himself with nothing more than his faith, Martin Luther was ready for battle.

Chapter 4 – The Diet of Worms and the War of Words

"We must make a great difference between God's Word and the word of man. A man's word is a little sound, that flies into the air, and soon vanishes. But the Word of God is greater than heaven and Earth. Yea, greater than death and hell. For it forms part of the power of God, and endures everlastingly."

Martin Luther

Prior to being summoned to present himself before the Imperial Diet of Worms for questioning, Martin Luther's safety had been assured by his local benefactor, the Elector of Saxony. He was nominally safe in the German states of the Holy Roman Empire, but making his way to Worms still presented some risk, a fact that was signaled by the Holy Roman Emperor ordering the seizure of certain texts Luther had written. The new emperor was apparently trying to play it safe lest the pope think he was being friendly with a known heretic.

Luther appeared before the Diet on April 17, 1521. The power of Luther's growing celebrity was once again proven at this event. It's said that the population of the city of Worms doubled due to the rush of spectators who simply wished to get a glimpse of the man who had stirred up so much controversy.

Unlike his other notorious engagements, however, Luther was not there to debate. During the Diet of Worms, Luther was expected to only speak when directly asked a question. When presented with his own written works, for example, he was asked, "Are these your books?" And when Luther confirmed that they were, he was then asked if he wished to renounce what he had written—which, of course, Luther refused to do.

Luther knew that this was coming and, in fact, had joked with one of his friends beforehand by remarking, "This shall be my recantation at Worms: 'Previously I said the pope is the vicar of Christ. I recant. Now I say the pope is the adversary of Christ and the apostle of the Devil.'" In other words, rather than apologizing and recanting his previous remarks, Luther intended to double down even further.

Despite his bombast before his arrival, once he was seated before high-ranking members of the clergy, Luther seemed to momentarily lose his nerve. In a shaky, morose sounding voice, Luther asked if he could be given a little while to consider the consequences. Ecken and his colleagues then discussed the matter, and though it was against Ecken's better judgment, they reached the consensus that Luther would be given some time to think it over. In fact, they gave him a whole day, dismissing the monk and instructing him to return the following day. Luther was at a crossroads and grappling with his own will. The future of the Reformation, in the meantime, would depend on what he decided to do next. After being allowed to sleep on it, Luther did indeed return to the diet the next day, on April 18. This time, he was taken to a much larger room that allowed for a bigger crowd to be assembled to watch the main event. Luther was once again subjected to several rounds of questioning, but he was notably calmer this time and seemed to be much better prepared for the occasion. He held fast to his previous teachings, explaining that his work typically fell into three categories. One category was his commentary on Scripture, another his critique of what he perceived to be errors of the Vatican, and the third was his writings directed at those who debated his theology.

The most ground Luther would give was in admitting that some of his treatises that criticized individual members of the clergy may have gone a little too far in their vitriolic nature. But although his choice of words could be a bit sensational at times, he maintained that their intention was good and the works themselves should not be banned. Luther stood by his work, although he acknowledged his own flawed character traits, admitting, "I do not set myself up as a saint."

Luther maintained that he only used such over-the-top language to get his point across when he felt that others needed to be corrected. He furthermore insisted that he was unable to recant of his previous writings because he truly believed the pope needed to be corrected of his idolatry and tyranny. He then challenged his interrogators by suggesting that if they could prove his writings contradicted Scripture, he would be the first to "cast them into the flames."

The main purpose of this supposed trial, however, was not so much to understand Luther's beliefs as it was to get him to recant from them. His interrogators were not in the least impressed by his interpretation of Scripture or philosophy. Ecken, weary of Luther's long replies, at one point bluntly informed him that "he doubted Luther had somehow discovered something new in Christianity after fifteen centuries of history."

As confrontational as this whole episode was, towards the end of his interrogation, Luther tried to strike a more conciliatory tone by suggesting that he welcomed the vigorous discussion that his words had caused. He declared, "I must say that for me it is a joyful spectacle to see that passions and conflicts arise over the Word of God. For that is how the Word of God works! As the Lord Jesus said, 'I came to send not peace, but a sword.'" Luther's words rubbed his interrogator, Johann von der Ecken, the wrong way, however, and Ecken even accused Luther of arrogant insolence in his remarks.

Ecken then demanded once again that Luther state whether he intended to recant or stand by his claims. After a moment, Luther issued his response. In words that would go down in history, he steadfastly declared, "Unless I am convicted by Scripture and plain reason—I do not accept the authority of popes and councils, for they have contradicted each other—my conscience is captive to the Word of God. I cannot and I will not recant anything, for to go against conscience is neither right nor safe. Here I stand. I cannot do otherwise. God help me. Amen."

Ecken slammed Luther as one who was attempting to pretend that he was wiser than all the teachers of the church and had a better knowledge of the Bible than they. Holy Roman Emperor Charles was not too impressed, either. Although he did indeed ensure Luther safe passage from the forum, the emperor made his displeasure known. He issued an official edict in which he declared that Luther was to be "held in detestation as a limb severed from the Church of God, the author of a pernicious schism, a manifest and obstinate heretic."

Such a decree put Luther in a very precarious position since just about anyone on the street willing to act out against him would now seem to have the full backing of not only the Catholic Church but also the Holy Roman Emperor. The Roman Emperor had guaranteed Luther safe passage, so he could not simply have one of his troops kill Luther, but nothing would stop a random passerby from doing the dirty work for him. Therefore, upon leaving the Diet of Worms, Luther had to be on guard lest he was seized by some Catholic zealot hell-bent on exacting vengeance for the pope.

Luther would not be assaulted during his trip back to Wittenberg. Instead, he would be intercepted by emissaries of his protector, the Elector of Saxony. These men staged a kidnapping to bring Luther directly under their protective custody. Luther was held at Wartburg (German for "Watch Tower") Castle, where under the care of his powerful friend, he set to work translating the Bible into German—a translation in which Luther would later relegate traditional books he felt were less inspired, such as the book of James, Hebrews, and even the prophetic text of Revelation, to an appendix in the back.

Most important for the movement, however, was his decision to do away with Old Testament books such as the book of Maccabees, since it was from this book that the Catholic Church pointed to verses that seemed to justify their concepts of both purgatory and indulgences. Later Protestant Bibles would continue to omit Maccabees but would go against Luther's directive to minimize the importance of books such as James, Hebrews, and Revelation, allowing them to remain intact.

Holed up in Warburg Castle, Martin Luther grew his hair out, dressed as a knight, and went by the name of "Junker Jorg," or "Knight George." Meanwhile, back at Wittenberg University, Luther's followers were attempting to continue the reform that Luther had begun. Leading this group of young scholars was a young man by the name of Philipp Melanchthon.

Philipp tried to hold his own in the Reformation movement, but he was eventually too overwhelmed by the more conservative forces at work and was effectively silenced. But thankfully for the movement, one of Philipp's colleagues, a certain Professor Andreas Karlstadt, mustered up the fortitude to continue. It was Karlstadt that started taking some of Luther's ideas and putting them into practice, such as refraining from making use of the traditional vestments of a priest when conducting mass.

Karlstadt would also later (and rather dramatically) put another of Martin Luther's objections to Catholic tradition to practice by taking back his vow of celibacy and marrying a young woman by the name of Anna von Mochau, whom he wed in January of 1522. Although still a celibate monk himself at the time, Luther did indeed object to the idea that priests needed to be celibate. Luther had declared that such man-made vows were a "vain attempt to win salvation" and were ultimately illegitimate and false.

With his marriage to Anna von Mochau, Karlstadt showed that he wholeheartedly agreed with Luther's assessment. Martin Luther himself would eventually get married, as well. One can understand later criticisms of Luther from the Catholic Church by those who felt that he was simply some lustful monk that wanted to get married. But this, of course, glosses over the fundamental flaws that Luther saw in church teaching at the time. Luther didn't want to just break tradition and do as he pleased—he had some serious issues with the Catholic Church's teachings.

Although Luther initially just wanted to reform the Catholic Church, the Reformation would take on a militant shape that he could hardly have envisioned. Early in his stay at Castle Wartburg, he heard of various doctrinal splits and sects coming into existence. The theological clashes were creating stress not only for clergy but also for local political leadership since the turmoil of pro-Reformation and anti-Reformation sects was often so volatile it verged on violence.

Martin Luther's personal protector, Prince Frederick, feared that the situation would become too chaotic for him to maintain governance. Luther even expressed alarm at what was transpiring. At one point, he wrote down his thoughts, stating, "I have been waiting for Satan to attack this sensitive spot—but he decided not to make use of the papists. Now he is making efforts in and among us evangelicals to produce the worst conceivable schism. May Christ quickly trample him under his feet."

Martin Luther seemed to believe that the chaotic forces he helped to unleash were somehow of satanic influence. Hearing of the turmoil, Luther could no longer stand idly by, and despite the risk to his own personal wellbeing, he left his exile in Castle Wartburg and made his way back to Wittenberg University in the spring of 1522.

Upon his return to Wittenberg, Luther set about trying to restore some semblance of peace. He delivered several sermons, referred to as his "Invocavit Sermons," named as such since they began on Invocate Sunday, the first Sunday of Lent. In Luther's remarks, he made it clear he believed that some of his followers were taking things too far. He stressed that reform needed to be a gradual, slow process—not outright revolutionary change. Luther maintained that Christians needed to be slowly guided out of the old ways of the church. As he put it, "No one should be dragged to them [the Catholic Church] or away from them by the hair, for I can drive no man to heaven or beat him into it with a club."

At this time, Luther found himself at odds with his former ally Karlstadt, who he immediately banned from the pulpit and denounced as a "rebellious, murderous, seditious spirit." Karlstadt seems to have taken the reforms of Luther too far and too fast for its author to handle. Karlstadt, nonplussed by Luther's reaction, quickly labeled Luther as nothing more than a half-hearted reformer who was no better than the pope.

Luther also took issue with certain reforms that Karlstadt was attempting to make. Luther especially despised Karlstadt's decision to do away with infant baptism. Luther had learned long ago as an Augustinian monk that all are born with the stain of original sin and believed that infant baptism was necessary to remove it. Luther would cling to this belief for the rest of his life, and as it pertained to at least this ancient practice of the church, he defied any reformer who attempted to omit it.

Martin Luther fought Karlstadt tooth and nail over this and many other issues. At the cost of a former friend and ally, Luther reestablished himself as the leader of the movement. Under Luther's much more steady hand, the situation in Wittenberg was once again under control. But soon enough, the tremors of the Reformation would break through new ground further afield, and even the skillful oratory of Martin Luther would not be able to so easily constrain it.

In Switzerland, for example, a prominent rival had arisen in the form of a Swiss preacher named Huldrych Zwingli. It was in 1522, during Lent, that Zwingli bucked tradition in a big way by simply hosting a gathering in which parishioners ate sausage. This might sound almost humorous today, but at the time, it was a big deal since it broke the traditional stipulation of not eating meat prior to Easter.

Reformers like Zwingli tapped into the popular local sentiment in which people (Germanic peoples, especially) wished to override some of the practice forced on them by the Roman Catholic Church and bring back local cultural traditions. They were going to eat sausage whether the Pope condemned them for it or not. Luther was no doubt the inspiration for this sudden defiance.

Another direct offshoot of the Reformation Luther had begun was a local preacher by the name of Thomas Müntzer. Müntzer had been a follower of Luther who took up an early interest in his teachings. In fact, it was Luther who had installed Thomas Müntzer as a priest at Zwickau in 1520. Thomas wished to move at a much faster pace than Luther, however, and he consequently found himself at odds with both Luther and the Catholic Church.

Due to the discord that had emerged, it wasn't long before Thomas Müntzer turned his back on Luther altogether. He began to criticize Luther for not accepting his prophetic vision. Feeling that Luther was a bit too comfortable to be the revolutionary religious leader the people needed, Müntzer began to deride Martin Luther, calling him "Brother Fattened Swine" and "Brother Soft Life."

Not only that, Müntzer began to advocate the violent overthrow of those whom he felt were not doing enough to reform the Catholic Church. At one point, Thomas Müntzer unabashedly declared, "The angels who sharpen their sickles for the cutting are the earnest servants of God who fulfill the zeal of divine wisdom." It was this one radical reformer—Thomas Müntzer— and his militancy that would eventually lead to an all-out war.

Chapter 5 – The Reformation Heats Up

"If anyone attempted to rule the world by the gospel and to abolish all temporal law and sword on the plea all are baptized and Christian, and that according to the gospel, there shall be among them no law or sword—or need for either—pray tell me, friend, what would he be doing? He would be loosing the ropes and chains of the savage wild beasts and letting them bite and mangle everyone, meanwhile insisting that they were harmless, tame, and gentle creatures; but I would have the proof in my wounds. Just so would the wicked under the name of Christian abuse evangelical freedom, carry on their rascality, and insist that they were Christians subject neither to law nor sword, as some are already raving and ranting."

Martin Luther

The radical reformer, Thomas Müntzer, wished to bring change far faster than Martin Luther would have liked. The former pupil slammed Luther as being soft and demanded that he develop a more aggressive stance against Catholic teaching. It was in castigation of this supposed softness that Müntzer wrote up the tract "A Highly Provoked Defense and Answer to the Spiritless, Soft-living Flesh at Wittenberg who Has Most Lamentably Befouled

Pitiable Christianity in a Perverted Way by His Theft of Holy Scripture."

Thomas Müntzer, on the other hand, advocated open violence and destruction that led to widescale rioting in which both churches and clergy were attacked. In 1524, Müntzer found his way to the city of Mühlhausen in the region of Thuringia, where he met up with a fellow zealous reformer by the name of Heinrich Pfeiffer and crafted a list of demands called the "Eleven Mühlhausen Articles," in which the pair tried to pressure local governance to better match their interpretation of what they called biblical truth.

Müntzer's pushes for revolutionary reform would eventually lead to the terrible infighting of 1525, known as the Peasants' War. The Peasants' War was a grassroots uprising of the peasant class against not only the Catholic Church but also the entire landed gentry—it was just as much an economic/political war as it was a religious one. The downtrodden peasants were trying to use Martin Luther's teaching against certain Catholic Church regulations as a reason to overthrow all hold the status quo had on them.

This phenomenon terrified Martin Luther, who quickly sought to distance himself from it. Shortly after the disturbance erupted, Luther published a tract in which he openly called for the destruction of those involved, referring to the radicals as nothing more than "robbing and murdering hordes of peasants." It must be remembered that, although Luther was in rebellion against some elements of the mainstream, such as the Roman Catholic Church (and perhaps the Holy Roman Emperor), he was largely backed by the German nobility. His number one ally, after all, was the Elector of Saxony.

Martin Luther, therefore, wasted no time in siding with the upper classes in this case and made it known that he wished for the disturbance to immediately cease. Luther's wishes would be fulfilled when the uprising was squashed and Thomas Müntzer himself was hauled into custody and executed. Müntzer had attempted to spark a larger rebellion in the region of Thuringia, but many of the peasantry abandoned the cause when the regional powers rallied against them.

Of those who decided to remain, some 6,000 were killed and another 600 taken captive. Among those taken prisoner were Thomas Müntzer and Heinrich Pfeifer; both were tortured and forced to recant. Their heads were then chopped off and impaled on pikes.

Luther had begun his protestations against the Catholic Church in opposition to heavy-handedness, yet when it came to those who were too radical for his taste, he viewed their annihilation as quite justifiable. As expressed in his "Against the Robbing and Murdering Hordes of Peasants," he maintained, "It is just as when one must kill a mad dog; if you do not strike him, he will strike you, and a whole land with you." Ironically, Catholic authorities, as well as Protestant ones, began to use Martin Luther's own words as a justification to squash Reformation-inspired peasant rebellions of all kinds. It is indeed ironic that Luther, a man who kicked off a desire to pull away from authoritarian religious doctrine, began to openly denounce those he disagreed with—or even those who just happened to disagree with him!

This was indicated when, shortly after his publication of Against the Murderous, Thieving Hordes of Peasants, he wrote an open letter to the previous text in which he ominously proclaimed, "I must warn those who criticize my book to hold their tongues and to be careful not to make a mistake and lose their own heads." Luther was obviously ready to not only verbally combat his opponents but render physical force if need be.

In Switzerland, meanwhile, Huldrych Zwingli was making some major waves. In 1522, he had weighed in on a controversy regarding fasting during Lent. Several parishioners had decided to break the rule to abstain from meat, and Zwingli supported their decision. He even published a tract about it called "The Freedom of Choice in the Selection of Food."

In this work, Huldrych Zwingli insisted that "fasting was a human tradition, not a divine injunction, and therefore was a question for the conscience of the individual Christian, not a matter which the authorities should legislate." Zwingli also was quite adept at using Scripture to justify his arguments—so much so that local officials decided to reform the rules pertaining to Lent if the religious orthodoxy could not find equally compelling scriptural arguments to back up their traditions.

After artfully laying out why dietary habits should not be controlled by the Catholic Church, Zwingli and his followers then moved on to tackle the argument over the veneration of saints. Zwingli opposed it. Zwingli also challenged the Catholic practice of enforcing celibacy among the priesthood. Zwingli insisted that since early church leaders such as the Apostle Peter had been married, there was no reason to issue a blanket ban on marriage upon the clergy. The argument was a personal one for Huldrych Zwingli since he was part of a clandestine marriage of his own—wed to a widow by the name of Anna Reinhart.

It's important to note that Martin Luther also took a wife around this time. His marriage stemmed from a rather dramatic episode in 1523 when he aided the escape of a nun named Katharina von Bora from a convent. As it turns out, Katharina was not in the convent by choice but was placed there by her father shortly after her mother had passed away. Her father eventually remarried, and Katharina was left in the convent simply for the convenience of her father. Hearing of the plight of this unhappy nun, Luther helped Katharina and eleven other nuns leave the convent that was holding them by smuggling the sisters out of the place in herring barrels.

After securing her release, Martin Luther placed Katharina in the care of a prominent lawyer named Philip Reichenbach. Katherina was in her mid-twenties at the time, and back in the 1500s, the options for a young woman like Katherina were rather limited. Since most women were not allowed to be their own breadwinners, typically the best route for security was through marriage. Luther found himself in the role of matchmaker, trying to introduce Katharina to potential suitors who could give her a home.

The suitors Luther provided all fell through, however. In the meantime, Luther, who was in his forties at the time, found himself falling in love with Katherina. This growing fondness culminated in their marriage on June 13, 1525. Other Protestants followed the example of both Martin Luther and Huldrych Zwingli as it pertained to celibacy and the right of Christians to marry.

At any rate, the common theme of all the arguments Zwingli raised was that the Bible should be the ultimate authority of Christian life and not the Roman Catholic Church or local governing officials. This view, which was indeed on par with Martin Luther's and was clearly explained in Huldrych Zwingli's The Clarity and Certainty of the Word of God. In a similar fashion to Martin Luther, he also delivered up theses. Yes, just like Luther had dished out his Ninety-five Theses, Zwingli crafted his own Sixty-Seven Articles, in which he went to great lengths to explain where he felt the Church needed serious reform.

It was in 1525 that Zwingli and his followers achieved a major success when the local city council of Zurich decided to formally abolish the requirement of mass—allowing citizens to carry out communion services in their own fashion and, more importantly, in their own language. Rather than Latin, which most Swiss didn't understand, services could now be held in German. Huldrych Zwingli had achieved meaningful reform through peaceful means, even as Müntzer's peasant revolt was going down in flames.

But Zwingli's efforts would not remain bloodless ones. The first major sign of discord in Zwingli's Reformation was when a group of fellow Swiss reformers decided that they didn't want to follow the Catholic tradition of baptizing infants. They argued that the New Testament Christians never had infants baptized, only adults. Therefore, they determined that only adults should be baptized in their day, as well. Like Martin Luther before him, Huldrych Zwingli apparently considered this too extreme of a position to take.

Zwingli wished to keep the baptism practice the Catholic Church already had in place and derided the baptismal reformers as "anti-baptists," or as they would later be known, "Anabaptists." To Zwingli's great dismay, however, Anabaptist ideology began to catch on in the Swiss city of Zurich, leading some parents to refuse to have their babies baptized. As lay preachers rose to baptize or re-baptize adult Christians, Zwingli questioned the motives of the instigators.

Rather than feeling their efforts were divinely inspired, Zwingli came to believe that these were just attention-getters who had a measureless thirst for fame. Things then took a rather ugly turn in 1526 when the local government attempted to thwart the movement by declaring that anyone who persisted in defying official Church doctrine on baptism would be put to death by drowning. This is said to have been "a form of punishment deliberately chosen to mock Anabaptist practice."

Although Zwingli had denounced the more radical Swiss reformers, soon after a major crackdown on the Anabaptists he, too, was called into question. He was asked to meet with none other than Johann Eck, who had questioned Luther at the Diet of Worms, to speak at a similar disputation in the Swiss city of Baden. Unlike Luther, who had met the challenge delivered to him by Eck, Zwingli refused, and this refusal alone was enough to have him labeled a heretic.

This meant that all of Zwingli's previously written works were now considered heretical, as well. Although Zwingli was not exactly a militant before, after he was condemned a heretic, he would certainly become one. Unlike the Anabaptists, who tended to suffer as persecuted pacifists, he was ready to lead an aggressive faction of Swiss reformers.

Martin Luther, for his part, was by now just as much against Zwingli as the Catholics were. In his 1528 piece entitled Confession Concerning Christ's Supper, he quite unabashedly declared, "I regard Zwingli as an un-Christian, with all his teaching, for he holds and teaches no part of the Christian faith rightly. He is seven times worse than when he was a papist." These were pretty harsh words from a man who had been so severely persecuted for his own beliefs.

Zwingli ultimately met his end on October 11, 1531, when a Catholic army was raised against him and his reformers in Zurich. Huldrych Zwingli himself is said to have died on the battlefield with a sword in hand—very much living up to Jesus' cautioning admonition that "those who live by the sword" would also surely "die by the sword." It is said that the Catholic troops who came across Zwingli's mortally-wounded form attempted to show mercy by offering Zwingli the chance to partake in the last rites of a Catholic believer. Zwingli had not become a reformer to turn back at the last minute, however. Instead, Huldrych Zwingli refused and was delivered a mortal blow by one of the troop's swords. As a final insult, it is said that they then burned his body and had his ashes sprinkled over the excrement of pigs. It was indeed a terrible end for this would-be reformer. At the height of his reformation efforts, Zwingli had envisioned an entire Christian confederation, in which a reformed church could be established, being created in Switzerland. His death, however, managed to crush his burgeoning movement in Zurich. With Huldrych Zwingli's death, Martin Luther remained the best-known middle-of-the-road reformer.

Chapter 6 – From Melchiorite to Mennonite—Some Additional Strains of Reformation

"Scholars have argued that without humanism the Reformation could not have succeeded, and it is certainly difficult to imagine the Reformation occurring without the knowledge of languages, the critical handling of sources, the satirical attacks on clerics and scholastics, and the new national feeling that a generation of humanists provided. On the other hand, the long-term success of the humanist owed something to the Reformation. In Protestant schools and universities classical culture found a permanent home."

Steven Ozment

As Martin Luther stayed the course in Wittenberg, more radical sects continued to sprout up all around him. In 1533, the Netherlands saw a brief but incredibly dramatic movement emerge under the leadership of a German furrier by the name of Melchior Hoffman. Known as Melchiorism, this reform movement preached an apocalyptic vision of the "imminent return" of Christ.

At one point, Hoffman even came to believe a fellow prophetic visionary who informed him that Christ would return once Melchior was arrested and thrown in prison. It's hard to fathom how his arrest would trigger the Second Coming, but Melchior seemed to be an enthusiastic supporter of the notion, and as such, he went out of his way to fulfill the prophecy by getting arrested before the year was out.

The original prophecy claimed that Christ would return after Melchior was imprisoned for six months. But, as far as anyone can tell, Christ didn't return in 1533, and rather than being released after six months, Melchior died in prison several years later. After Melchior was out of the picture, the next leader of the so-called Melchiorites was a man named Jan Mathijs. Under the leadership of Jan Mathijs, the Melchiorites set up a base in the region of Westphalia (northwestern Germany), in the town of Münster.

Anabaptists also increasingly flocked to the city and began to call it their "New Jerusalem." It wasn't long before tensions among Luther's followers, the Melchiorites, Anabaptists, Catholics, and others became incredibly strained. Followers of Martin Luther—Lutherans—were suspected of being in league with Catholic authorities, and the Anabaptists and Melchiorites began to fear that the Lutherans would send in the Catholic troops to annihilate them.

Things came to a head when the Anabaptists, under the leadership of one Hermann Redeker, converged on city hall en masse, brandishing swords. The local Catholic bishop sent a small militia to engage the reformers, and the show of force convinced them to sue for peace. As soon as the truce was declared, however, the Melchiorite Jan Mathijs moved in and reestablished his own power base. Mathijis is said to have become so influential in the city at one point that he convinced city authorities to persecute and imprison his rivals.

However, Jan's reign came to an end when, after having a dream in which he was victorious against the Catholic army, he charged off to face Catholic troops—who easily dispatched with the zealous reformer. It was after the death of Jan Mathijs that another Melchiorite, a man named Jan van Leiden, took over the Münster movement. Jan van Leiden had tremendous sway over Münster's city council, so much so that he was eventually able to get the city council dismissed outright.

Then, in the fall of 1534, van Leiden unabashedly declared Münster to be a theocracy under his guidance. This radical reformer declared that he had been given power over emperors, kings, princes, and all the power of the Earth. In his power trip, Jan van Leiden sought to liken himself to King David or King Solomon, ruling over a religious city-state. His most faithful followers sought to confirm this claim of authority by issuing a prediction that their so-called King Jan would eventually take over the Earth in its entirety, and eliminate his rivals.

It's hard to believe that Luther's initial calls for reformation could lead to such radical developments, and Luther himself was perhaps more dumbfounded by this development than anyone else. Luther had hoped to create a united Protestant front but ended up facing the reality that his break with the Catholic Church had led to several others rising to thrust forth their own unique interpretations of Scripture—which were just as often contrary to as inspired by his own teachings.

Martin Luther must have realized that the great strength of the Catholic Church was its dogged quest for uniformity since he now had to endure the rise of a seemingly endless variety of factions and denominations coming to fruition. The most Luther could settle for was his own Protestant brand, which had become known as Lutheranism, to carry the torch of his teachings. Most galling, however, was the fact that Luther, who was initially persecuted by the Catholic Church for deviating from official Church doctrine, found himself having to encourage persecution of rival sects that he had found to be dangerously heretical.

He encouraged the squashing of the peasant rebellion, the Anabaptists, and many others who ideologically rubbed him the wrong way. By being an authoritarian controller of what he viewed to be correct doctrine, was Luther becoming the very thing he hated when he rebelled against the Roman Catholics in the first place? Yet for Luther, heavy-handed crackdowns were preferable to having to deal with some of the more radical results of the Reformation.

The previously mentioned King Jan, for example, had begun running the city of Münster as a dictator. Other Protestants viewed one of King Jan's most egregious actions to be the use of Old Testament Scripture to justify polygamous marriages. Thanks to the support of Jan van Leiden, these polygamous unions were among the first the Christian world had seen. King Jan not only allowed polygamous marriage but belligerently enforced the practice when church members objected.

One woman, for example, objected to her husband having more than one wife and was consequently executed. King Jan was even known to have executed a spouse or two of his own on similar grounds. According to Reformation scholar and writer Andrew Atherstone, when it was all said and done, the poor "citizens of Münster lived in abject fear under this Melchiorite reign of terror."

With such absolute anarchy erupting in certain Reformation circles, Luther saw no clear alternative to this chaos except to vigorously fight back against views he considered heretical. As for King Jan, his so-called tyrannical reign came to an end on June 25, 1535, when Catholic troops were brought forward to crush yet another Protestant insurgency. In the aftermath, it is said that Münster's streets were strewn with corpses and awash with blood.

As for King Jan? He, like so many other radical reformers, paid the ultimate price—he was taken out to the "Münster market." This was the sort of place one could find a butcher in a stall slicing up fresh slabs of meat for eager customers. But it wasn't animal flesh that was butchered at the market on that day—it was King Jan. He was brutally tortured by having his flesh ripped apart with red-hot iron tongs.

The pain must have been unbearable, and King Jan was only relieved of it when his throat was slit and a knife was shoved into his heart. After being killed in this manner, he and the bodies of two of his compatriots were placed in iron cages and hung from the steeple of Münster's now-infamous landmark—St. Lambert's Church. Although the mortal remains of Jan and company are long gone, the iron cages remain suspended as an ominous warning to this very day.

After this latest militant strain of Anabaptists was put to rest, a newly-christened pacifist group that would become known as the Mennonites would take root. The Mennonites were founded by a former Catholic priest named Menno Simmons. Menno joined the Melchiorites in 1536, and he rose to leadership of the movement in 1540. Soon thereafter, his followers ceased to be known as Melchiorites and instead were referred to as Mennonites.

Menno made his way through much of northern Germany and the Netherlands, preaching his doctrine on baptism and the power of faith. But the big difference between the Mennonites and the Melchiorites was the fact that the Mennonites were taught to spread their message through pacifistic means. Rather than taking over city councils and trying to govern communities, the Mennonites (much like the early Christians) simply sought to change the hearts and minds of those who heard them—persuading them through preaching rather than force.

Even though other Protestants and Catholics still disagreed with much of the Mennonite teaching, you would think they would at least appreciate the non-violent nature of the Mennonite movement. Yet, Holy Roman Emperor Charles V made it his personal mission to stamp the Mennonites out and even offered a reward should someone bring Mennonite leader Menno into his custody.

Needless to say, the Mennonites did not have the powerful political backers that Martin Luther did. Martin Luther was a true power broker in his day and, in many ways, was viewed as a kind of "Protestant pope" in the way that he could effectively maneuver through all the intrigue between the Catholic Church and rival Protestant groups. And Luther's views of the Mennonites were not too encouraging. He viewed them as schismatic heretics who consigned children to hell since they refused to engage in infant baptism.

With both Catholics and Lutherans against them, the Mennonites were persecuted so badly that, for most of them, the only real option was to flee. The Mennonite diaspora would have these Protestant reformers traveling far and wide. A new base was found for some time in the Netherlands, and eventually, many more would migrate all the way across the Atlantic Ocean to America, where Mennonite communities can still be found. From Melchiorite to Mennonite, this tradition sprung from the Reformation remains strong.

Chapter 7 – England's Reformation Begins

"Alas, how can the poor souls live in concord when you preachers sow amongst them in your sermons debate and discord? They look to you for light and darkness. Amend these crimes, I exhort you, and set forth God's word truly, both by true preaching and giving a good example, or else I, whom God has appointed his vicar and high minister here, will see these divisions extinct, and these enormities corrected."

King Henry VIII

As the Reformation unfolded on the European continent, across the English Channel, a British king called Henry VIII was paying very close attention to the developments. As Henry saw the propagation of Protestant faith across Europe, he initially saw it as his chance to present himself as a stalwart defender of Catholicism against the newfound heretics. And he wasted no time in doing it.

Just a short time after Martin Luther's infamous showdown at the Diet of Worms in 1521, in fact, King Henry VIII put together a carefully worded "doctrinal treatise" in which he took Martin Luther's beliefs to task. A hallmark of Lutheran belief stemmed from Luther's work—The Babylonian Captivity of the Church—in which the reformer maintained that the only two sacraments that mattered were the Lord's Supper and baptism.

Henry was a fierce opponent of this assertion, standing by the Catholic Church's seven standard sacraments. King Henry VIII wrote a polemical text called Assertio Septem Sacramentorum (Defense of the Seven Sacraments), in which he made his beliefs on this matter crystal clear. He also made his distaste of Luther obvious when he declared that he was nothing more than "a knavish little friar."

Among other things, Henry also described Luther as being one who "spews out viper's venom" and was leading the whole flock astray. All of this, of course, was music to the Roman Catholic pope's ears. Luther may have secured his physical protection through the Elector of Saxony, but he was not out of the reach of King Henry VIII's full-on bombastic verbal assault. The pope was so happy, in fact, that he officially bestowed upon King Henry the title of "Fidei Defensor," or "Defender of the Faith."

The official faith of England at this time, of course, was the Roman Catholic religion. Yes, even though King Henry eventually kicked off his own reformation in England, in the early days of the Protestant Reformation, he was indeed a defender of the Catholic faith. But even though Henry cast himself as the defensive wall against the epidemic of European Protestantism, some strains of the movement did indeed seep through to the British Isles.

Martin Luther's works were being translated into various languages at a rapid clip, and some of them found their way to English shores. One of the places where these migratory theological works surfaced was none other than Cambridge. Here it is said that the works were well received by the colleagues of a certain Thomas Bilney. Bilney had gone through his own period of reform when he read a recently translated copy of the New Testament in which the words of Saint Paul, which declared "that Christ Jesus came into the world to save sinners, of whom I am the worst," struck him to the core.

Bilney was moved by the concept that even one of the Bible's greatest saints considered himself one of the worst. If even Paul could do nothing to save himself, it only seemed to clarify the Protestant teaching that works are meaningless and it is only through faith that one can be saved. Bilney began to openly speak of what he had learned with others at Cambridge, and soon many of his associates were also moved to reconsider Catholic teachings.

During this same time, a British scholar named William Tyndale began to work on developing a new translation of the Bible that did not depend on the Catholic Church's Latin translation but rather the original Hebrew and Greek languages it was written in. It was a major undertaking—one you might think his countrymen would have been proud of—but according to an English law called the Constitutions of Oxford, written back in 1408, it was considered illegal for such a translation to be made.

It may seem a bit bizarre that it would be illegal to merely develop a new translation of the Bible, but this was indeed the case. Knowing that his work could get him in some real hot water in England, Tyndale hightailed out of Britain and made his way to Luther's backyard—arriving first in Cologne, and then the city of Worms. It was while in Worms that Tyndale managed to finish his translation of the New Testament in its entirety in 1526.

With his new translation in hand, Tyndale took full advantage of the printing press and began to print out several copies, which made their way to Britain. It's amazing to think that a Bible printed in one's own language would be so controversial, but for the Catholic Church, it was a very serious matter. As soon as Catholics in Britain got wind of what was happening, they did everything they could to seize the new translations making their way to Britain and have them burned.

Yes, it's absurd to think of Catholic priests burning Bibles, but that is indeed what happened. Tyndale was also thoroughly condemned by the Catholic scholar, Bishop Tunstall, who supposedly studied Tyndale's translated text and declared that there were some 2,000 errors in his translation. Citing these supposed errors, Bishop Tunstall demanded that all copies of the Tyndale translations be found and destroyed lest they lead the faithful astray.

Tyndale's Bible translation was indeed at odds with the traditional Latin translation of the Catholic Church. The Greek word metanoeo, which the Latin version understood as "penance," was translated into English as "repent." This slight change was very significant since it seemed to undermine the Catholic belief in having to do penance—an integral part of the Catholic faith. Incensed by these "dangerous translations," prominent statesmen and cardinal Thomas Wolsey led the charge of a massive search for biblical books and people associated with their circulation.

Books burned, and several went to prison in this effort to stamp out the newly-translated texts. Among those taken into custody over these heretical translations was a British scholar named John Frith. Frith was only let go after promising to stay within ten miles of Oxford. But Frith wasn't going to follow these orders and instead left Britain altogether, settling in Antwerp where Tyndale had taken up residence.

It was during this exile that Frith wrote the important reformatory text, the Disputation of Purgatory divided into Three Books, in which he presented his opinion that purgatory was an erroneous Catholic teaching. Tyndale also hammered away at Catholic doctrine with his own Protestant texts, largely patterned after Luther's original argument that Christians are saved by faith rather than works. Tyndale made the most waves when he wrote his seminal work, The Obedience of a Christian Man.

In this work, Tyndale made it clear that he believed man's ultimate allegiance should not be to a king or any government, but to God alone. The establishment did not like this at all since they believed Tyndale's liberating doctrine would spread dissent and rebellion among the masses. However, Tyndale deflected criticism by pointing out that, although he argued that man's ultimate allegiance was to God, the Bible was clear in its directive to submit to local governance.

Meanwhile, Tyndale absolutely excoriated Catholic priests for what he perceived to be their preoccupation with rituals and tradition. He sarcastically referenced their reverence for "holy water, holy fire, holy bread, holy salt, hallowed bells, holy wax, holy boughs, holy candles, and holy ashes" while presenting an apparent disregard for the Bible. His critics, on the other hand, maintained that the average person would not be able to understand Scripture unless it was filtered through the official interpretation sanctioned by the Catholic Church.

Tyndale wasn't buying it, however, and felt the Catholic Church was verging on a conspiratorial cover-up in its refusal to allow the English people to read Bibles translated into their own language. Tyndale claimed that Rome was purposefully keeping the British faithful in the dark and stated, "To keep us from knowledge of the truth, they do all things in Latin. They pray in Latin, they christen in Latin, they bless in Latin, they give absolution in Latin: only curse they in the English tongue."

In his attacks on the clergy, Tyndale also made an appeal directly to the king of England to weigh in on the controversy. Using a similar strategy as the German reformers, Tyndale sought to stir up national sentiment in the kingdom against the intervention of Rome. But King Henry VIII, a strong critic of Luther who had just been honored by the pope as the "Defender of the Faith," had yet to be swayed.

Mirroring Tyndale's efforts of persuasion, another British reformer in exile named Simon Fish wrote a piece called A Supplication for the Beggars, which he presented as an actual complaint from the blind, the sick, and the lame lodged against the invasion of England by a multitude of ecclesiastics who had come down on Britain like "ravenous wolves." Fish's bombastic tract urged that these interlopers be driven out and "whipped naked through every market town."

But King Henry was indeed on the side of Catholic hardliners at this point, and rather than drive out the Catholic clergy, he allowed his minions to do their best to drive out the Protestant reformers. Now, books were not the only thing burned, but in many cases, individuals went up in flames, as well. When caught, reformers were threatened with being burned at the stake, and under the terrible duress of torture, some were forced to recant.

One of the most famous to retract his Protestant beliefs under this pressure was Thomas Bilney, who caved and offered a full recantation in 1527 when confronted by Wolsey. His life was spared, but he would live to regret it. Unable to simply go back to his old way of life, Bilney broke down in 1531 and began to preach his views in the countryside of Norwich. Here he came upon a former nun converted to Protestantism and handed her a translated text of Tyndale's New Testament.

This bold act alerted the authorities and led to Bilney being burned at the stake shortly thereafter. The execution of Bilney seemed to kick off a spate of hardline crackdowns that lasted from late 1531 on into 1532. The persecution was so intense that, at one point, even people who were already dead were being burned at the stake. This was the case with William Tracy, who made his allegiance clear on his deathbed by refusing Catholic tradition and proclaiming "I accept none in heaven or in earth to be mediator between me and God, but only Jesus Christ."

This meant that Tracy denied the Catholic Church the chance to perform his last rites and died (albeit of natural causes) a heretic in the eyes of the Church. Since he was already dead, the Church had to settle for desecrating his corpse to set an example. So, his body was dug up and posthumously burned in effigy. It was during this purge of Protestants that John Frith was finally captured in 1531. Frith was immediately sent to London's Tower—that medieval dungeon of a holding cell—to await the kangaroo court the Catholics called a trial.

While Frith was locked up, Tyndale wrote him words of encouragement, extolling the prisoner, "Your cause is Christ's gospel, a light that must be fed with [the] blood of faith. Rejoice and be glad, for great is your reward in heaven." Frith stood trial shortly thereafter, and his chief prosecutor was a certain Bishop John Stokesley, who charged that Frith was nothing more than a "child of wickedness and darkness" and that he had committed the most detestable heresies. Stokesley also argued that Frith should receive the ultimate punishment, lest he "infect the Lord's flock with [his] heresy."

Until this point, the king of England, the man who had been hailed as the "Defender of the Faith" by the Catholic Church, had supported the hardline stance against the Reformation. But mitigating factors in the king's own life—or at least his marriage bed—would soon make the king change his stance dramatically. The king, who was at this point married to the Spanish princess, Katherine of Aragon, was desperate to have a male heir to the throne.

But, as of yet, his wife had only produced a daughter—Princess Mary. As the years went by and Katherine's miscarriages added up, King Henry became convinced that his wife would not be able to provide him with a male heir. Henry wanted to continue the Tudor line of which he was a part, and without a son he would not be able to do so. This put him in a terrible bind. He began to feel that his marriage was cursed. This is no exaggeration, since he took the words of Scripture in Leviticus (20:21) to heart. This verse of Scripture advised that, if a man were to marry his brother's wife, "it is an impurity."

King Henry had indeed married his brother's wife—at least, his former wife—since she was the widow of his brother, Prince Arthur. Henry began to openly wonder if this perceived violation of Leviticus could be the reason behind his troubles in securing a male heir. Since the Catholic Church generally forbade divorce, the king sought out ways in which the marriage might become annulled. The pope, however, refused to fulfill the king's wishes. This left the king scrambling to figure out an alternative. After consulting with Cardinal Wolsey and the pope's legate, Cardinal Campeggio, he was advised to have Katherine give up her marriage and join a convent so that Henry would be free to enter a new marriage.

As one might imagine, Katherine was not quite so thrilled with the prospect of stepping down as queen to become a nun. She was appalled at what was being suggested of her and sent a direct appeal to the pope. The king, in the meantime, was infuriated that his advisers were unable to find a better solution for him and had Cardinal Wolsey dismissed. He ended up with a new adviser who had been a previous associate of Wolsey, Thomas Cromwell.

It was Cromwell who began to conspire with the king about the possibility of using his own power to get what he wanted. The argument presented to Henry was twofold. It was determined that King Henry did indeed have solid reasoning to get an annulment due to the biblical grounds mentioned in Leviticus. Secondly, it was argued that papal authority could not command the king. King Henry always knew that he could try to force the issue, but, cherishing his role as "Defender of the Faith," he was hesitant to anger the pope.

Nevertheless, as he continued to consider increasing his powers and diminishing Rome's, Henry began to throw his weight around when it came to theological matters in England. In the spring of 1532, for example, he issued his "Supplication Against the Ordinaries," which argued that rather than the clergy deciding who would be charged with heresy, any such grievances needed to be directly addressed to King Henry.

Coming on the heels of the great persecution that had been launched in late 1531, this petition signaled a tremendous turnaround in England's handling of the Protestant Reformation. King Henry wasn't agreeing with the Protestants, but he was at least making the case that any grievances leveled against them should be brought to him before Roman Catholic clergy started lighting matches and burning folks at the stake.

Catholic clergy did not like this, however, and refused to recognize the decree. The following May, this led King Henry to declare, "We thought that the clergy of our realm had been our subjects wholly, but now we have well perceived that they be but half our subjects, yea, and scarce our subject: for all the prelates at their consecration make an oath to the pope, clear contrary to the oath that they make us, so they seem to be his subjects, and not ours."

These dire words were enough to get the clergy in line, and shortly thereafter, they formally conceded to royal decree, pledging that their actions would henceforth need to be justified by the king. In 1533, shortly after this recognition, King Henry finally made the move to put away his wife and remarry in complete defiance of the pope. His new Queen—Anne Boleyn—was decried as nothing more than a harlot in Catholic circles, but besides disparaging the union from afar, there was nothing the Roman Catholic clergy could do.

The king's power was then further cemented into British law in the fall of 1534 with the creation of the Act of Supremacy, which clearly stated that King Henry was to be considered the "only Supreme Head in Earth of the Church of England." According to this act, the king now had serious reformative power when it came to "all errors, heresies, and other enormities and abuses." Even though King Henry was previously against the Reformation, this act unilaterally made England a part of it since Henry managed to scale back any real power or control the pope had over English religious affairs.

Ironically enough, the king's break with Catholic authority led to a persecution of the very Catholic faithful of whom Henry had previously been dubbed the defender. For when Catholic diehards began to speak out against the king's actions, they—like the Protestants before them—ended up losing their lives. One of the most sensational of these persecutions of zealous Catholics occurred in April of 1534 when the so-called Holy Maid—a Catholic nun named Elizabeth Barton—was hung and decapitated for speaking out against the king.

In the early 1530s, Barton had made several prophesies about King Henry that were deemed seditious. She subsequently developed a brief following among English Catholics before being rounded up, tried for treason, and put to death for her beliefs. Many more executions followed in 1535, including some high-profile figures such as Cardinal John Fisher and Sir Thomas More—who were previously key players in the persecution and suppression of the Protestants.

Further internal reform of the Church of England took place in 1536, with new measures such as the insistence that the Ten Commandments be translated into English. It is rather stunning to think that men like Firth were killed over English translations of the Bible just a few years prior, only to have the king himself suddenly sanction the English translation of the Ten Commandments. The new regulations also criticized traditional Catholic practices such as "pilgrimages to local shrines [and] the offering of money or votive candles before religious relics," among other things.

But there was more to come. Going completely full circle in 1538, the king, who had previously turned a blind eye to the persecution of translators of the Bible, decreed that a full English translation should be openly distributed to church members. This led to the publication of the so-called Great Bible translation that was rendered by Miles Coverdale in April of 1539. This was the first authorized edition of the Bible—sanctioned by King Henry VIII himself.

The preface to the Great Bible, written by Archbishop Cranmer, urged the English to cherish the Scripture, stating that they were "a better jewel in our house than either gold or silver." This urging of the average Briton to have a Bible of their own was indeed a stark contrast to the previous years of hunting down anyone who so dared to read the Bible for themselves. It seemed that the king had put his finger on the scale for the Protestants after all, but it was a little more complicated than that.

While the king sought to present himself as the main authority for church doctrine rather than the pope, the old "Defender of the Faith" himself was still a stickler for many standard Catholic doctrines. The king had his own problems in the meantime. He had become increasingly paranoid as his inner circle conspired around him, so when Cromwell—seeking to rid himself of Queen Anne's influence—made up stories about her being unfaithful, the king took the bait.

Henry ended up having his own wife executed in 1536. It is incredibly cynical to consider it, but many have wondered if the king took this route as an expedient means of ridding himself of yet another wife who could not produce a son for him. Queen Anne had not yet been able to bear a son when she was beheaded. At any rate, upon her death, Henry wasted little time in taking a new wife—Jane Seymour.

It was Queen Jane who would finally give birth to the son that King Henry VIII so desperately craved. She gave birth to Prince Edward but, shortly thereafter, perished of septicemia, leaving the proud new father once again a widower. King Henry the VIII's next marriage would not be to bring about a son but was, instead, a marriage of political convenience.

Ever since England went rogue, there was a risk of Catholic powers such as France or the Holy Roman Empire deciding to intervene militarily. Although King Henry VIII had been initially against Martin Luther and all the other German reformers, he now saw them as potential allies. So, when the opportunity arose to marry a German noblewoman—Anne of Cleves—he agreed to do so out of sheer political pragmatism. However, the king was not too thrilled with his new wife and, at one point, even called her downright repulsive.

The marriage was annulled after just six months, in 1540. Shortly thereafter, the king tried his luck at marriage again by marrying Catherine Howard, the Duke of Norfolk's niece. This marriage wouldn't last very long, either. This queen proved to be rather scandalous and was caught having an affair with a man by the name of Thomas Culpeper. Both Catherine and Culpeper were executed for this offense, with Queen Catherine—the latest wife of King Henry to be beheaded—sent to the chopping block the day before St. Valentine's Day—February 13, 1542.

Shortly after the death of Catherine, King Henry seemed to have a change of heart regarding some of the religious liberty he had previously bestowed. In a complete reversal of his previously championing of Bible reading, he decided that not everyone should have access to Scripture. The king seemed to fear that too many people were getting the wrong ideas from Scripture and worried that it would lead to insurrection against him. As such, in 1543, he issued the Act for the Advancement of True Religion, which stipulated that there would be restrictions on who could read the Bible.

The act deemed that "women, servants, and laborers" should not be allowed to read Scripture on their own and furthermore dictated that they could be punished if found with their own translation of Scripture. Many English Protestants who were hopeful that the English king could lead them to a complete reformation of religion were greatly dismayed by the king's actions.

As the reformer John Hooper put it, "As far as true religion is concerned, idolatry is nowhere in greater vigor. Our king has destroyed the pope, but not popery. The impious mass, the most shameful celibacy of the clergy, the invocation of saints, auricular confession, superstitious abstinence from meats, and purgatory, were never before held by the people in greater esteem than at the present moment."

The king, meanwhile, had married for one final time in the summer of 1543 when he wed a widow by the name of Catherine Parr. Catherine herself was a supporter of the Reformation, and it is said that she continually tried to persuade her husband to be more supportive of the cause.

Henry was getting older, however, and seemed to be firmly stuck in his ways. Therefore, his strange hybrid form of anti-pope—yet still largely anti-Protestant doctrines—remained. And they would continue even some time after King Henry VIII's death in 1547. Martin Luther, the initial instigator of the Reformation, in the meantime, had died the prior year, in 1546. Both deaths would mark a sea change in the next phases of the larger Reformation.

Chapter 8 – The Rise of Calvinism

"When they inquire into predestination, let them remember that they are penetrating into the recesses of the divine wisdom, where he who rushes forward securely and confidently, instead of satisfying his curiosity will enter an inextricable labyrinth. For it is not right that man should with impunity pry into things that the Lord has been pleased to conceal within himself, and scan that sublime eternal wisdom that it is his pleasure that we should not apprehend but adore, that therein also his perfections may appear. Those secrets of his will, which he has seen it meet to manifest, are revealed in his word—revealed insofar as he knew to be conducive to our interest and welfare."

John Calvin

Second perhaps only to Martin Luther himself, one of the greatest forces at work in the Reformation was John Calvin. John— or as he was known to the French, Jean Cauvin—began his efforts at reform in France. It was during the persecution of Protestants in 1535 that Calvin fled France for Switzerland. Calvin first set up shop in the town of Basel. Here, he wrote long tracts about his religious theories, one of which was entitled The Institutes of the Christian Religion.

The book was dedicated to the then king of France—King Francois I—and included a heartfelt request for the king to put an end to his heavy-handedness against the Protestants of France. Calvin insisted that the Protestants were being maligned by their opponents, and requested an inquest into what he viewed as little more than a slander campaign. Another major argument that Calvin made was that the efforts of reformers were by no means a new invention.

Calvin made the case that what the reformers were attempting to accomplish was completely consistent with apostolic and early church doctrine. Furthermore, he made it known his position that he believed those who opposed the gospel—or at least his personal version of it—were "tools of Satan." It's not likely that Calvin's words addressed to the king had much impact, but as it so happens, the persecutions did come to a halt shortly thereafter: in the summer of 1535, the Edict of Coucy granted a general amnesty to the remaining Protestant reformers in France.

But this amnesty didn't come without a catch. As it stood, any and all who were deemed to be fugitives who had left France could only return and receive a pardon if they "renounced their heretical views within six months." The likes of hardline reformers such as John Calvin were obviously not going to suddenly renounce their so called heretical views simply to go back home. All John did was take advantage of the six-month grace period to return to France and take care of some personal matters.

But before this six-month window was out, John left France for good in 1536 rather than recant. He was only twenty-seven at the time and would live the rest of his years as a reformer in exile. After leaving France for the last time, he made his way to Geneva, Switzerland. Swiss cities had been home to several reform movements in the past, and Geneva had just passed legislation in

1536 ensuring the citizenry would be free of the authority of the Roman Catholic Church.

John Calvin began his work in Geneva by means of public lectures in which he argued his views on the Bible. Due to religious infighting, John Calvin was eventually expelled from Geneva in 1538. From there, he ended up in Strassburg, where he was made the pastor of a group of French-speaking Protestants. He was given this role by a prominent Protestant named Martin Bucer, who supposedly convinced John Calvin to take the position by reminding him of what happened to Jonah when he shirked the calling of God.

Jonah, according to Scripture, was the biblical prophet who was swallowed by a whale. Martin Bucer became John Calvin's number one advisor in all his affairs and eventually even turned into a matchmaker of sorts when he introduced John Calvin to an eligible widow named Idelette de Bure. Idelette had been a part of the Anabaptist faith that was dominant in Swiss cities at the time. After settling down in Strassburg, John Calvin began to write long treatises on his Protestant beliefs. Among them was his "Reply to Cardinal Sadoleto."

Written in 1539, this letter was indeed a reply to a certain Cardinal Sadoleto, who had previously crafted an open letter to reformers in Geneva, attempting to convince them to return to the Catholic faith. Sadoleto's letter stood out from other attempts to bring reformers back in line in that the cardinal's efforts seemed to be sincere—in fact, almost apologetic in nature—and openly admitted that the Roman Catholic Church did indeed need to face up to certain excesses and abuses of power.

But even given these concessions, Sadoleto tried to convince all who would read his words that there was still a place for them in the Roman Catholic Church. It's interesting to note that even though Calvin had been essentially run out of Geneva, he was still called upon at his new residence in Strassburg to answer the cardinal's entreaty. In his reply, Calvin hammered out the need for the Church to reform and made the case that the Reformation was not just about the abuses and corruption of the Church, but an effort to reform the "very heart" of Catholicism.

In this reply to Cardinal Sadoleto, Calvin went further than Martin Luther had in his Ninety-five Theses. When Martin Luther nailed his theses on that church door, he was indeed mainly seeking the reform of abuses and corruption of the Catholic Church, such as the sale of indulgences. Calvin, however, made it clear that he wasn't looking for reform as much as he was seeking revolution. He also made it clear that he and his associates were not "theological innovators" as detractors had charged, but rather, they were attempting to stay closer to the original principles of the New Testament than the Catholic Church had. During this time, he also wrote his own personal commentary on the New Testament book of Romans, as well as an extensive article that covered the Lord's Supper.

Close on the heels of these works, in 1540 and 1541, John Calvin and Martin Bucer toured the cities of Hagenau, Worms, and Regensburg, where they attended a series of theological debates that took place between Protestants and Catholics. Calvin found himself deeply disturbed by what he perceived as a terrible compromise in doctrine, amid the Protestants of Geneva. These divisions made him grow even more fond of the solidarity he had grown accustomed to in Strassburg.

John Calvin partially blamed the division he witnessed in Geneva on his own expulsion from the city. He knew this to be true, but all the same, when city authorities requested Calvin to return to his stewardship over the Protestant faithful, he claimed that he "shuddered at the very idea." This was the city that had thrown him out—why would he want to go back? Despite his misgivings, however, he finally did return as asked on September 13, 1541.

Calvin immediately set to work reforming the reformers, issuing his Ecclesiastical Ordinances in November of 1541. This work outlined Calvin's vision for how the church should be structured in Geneva and would eventually become a standard blueprint for many other churches far and wide. Calvin's church structure consisted of four primary roles in the church: deacons, elders, doctors, and pastors.

Calvin instructed his flock that pastors should corner the market when it came to preaching, spiritual counsel, and administration of sacraments. Doctors, on the other hand, should focus on matters of theology and engage in debates, lectures, or other similar speaking engagements. As for elders, Luther specifically instructed that there should be twelve elders selected from the laity. Deacons, meanwhile, were to focus on charity, such as aiding the impoverished and ill at health.

Beyond these directives for specific church roles, John Calvin's ordinances also reiterated his personal views on doctrinal issues such as baptism, the Lord's Supper, marriage, burial, visitation of the sick and prisoners, and the catechesis of children. As part of this new organization of the Protestants in Geneva, Calvin also established a council to oversee the whole of the operation. The council consisted of elders, pastors, and other church officials who routinely met and discussed the state of church affairs.

Often enough, this sort of religious oversight committee turned into nothing short of a tribunal when those accused of various sins they did not acknowledge or repent of were brought before the council for questioning. These sins ranged from adultery and blasphemy to simply accusations of being disrespectful in church. If those questioned refused to recant from their transgressions, they were suspended from the Lord's Supper, which essentially amounted to the Calvinist version of excommunication from the church.

To be clear, these were some fairly drastic reforms for many of Geneva's citizens, and not all supported them. One of Calvin's most prominent critics was a Swiss politician named Ami Perrin. Perrin objected to the scrutiny being placed upon everyone's personal lives and created a group of dissidents who went by the moniker of the "Children of Geneva." Due to their more liberal outlook, these objectors were later called the "Libertines."

Things came to a head when Ami Perrin's own spouse—Francoise—was brought before the council on charges of dancing. She was deemed guilty and thrown behind bars for the transgression. The situation was inflamed even further when the imprisoned woman's father was arrested for making remarks about Calvin being akin to "a Catholic priest at auricular confession who wanted to hear the details of everyone's sin."

John Calvin addressed some of the criticism being leveled at him in his 1550 work entitled On the Scandals that Today Prevent Many People from Coming to the Pure Doctrine of the Gospel and Ruin Others. Here Calvin was on both the defensive and offensive, as he defended his stance while simultaneously assaulting the character of those who dared disagree by calling them all a bunch of debauched fornicators who would rather follow the teachings of the pope than his recommended doctrine.

The strict oversight of Calvin's teaching was not the only thing that some objected to. For the more theologically minded, the most galling thing about Calvin wasn't that he didn't want people to dance—but rather that he believed everyone's ultimate destiny had already been determined. Known as predestination, this central tenant of Calvinism is the notion that God has determined ahead of time who goes to Heaven and who goes to hell. Today in Christian circles, the concept is usually mentioned with the more mundane vernacular of "once saved, always saved."

Even though Calvin had ignited a major debate over whether salvation is preordained by an all-knowing, omniscient God, the truth is, this debate has raged amongst Christians from the very beginning of Christianity. From the earliest of times, some Christians had believed that once you professed faith in Christ, absolutely nothing could take you out of his hand. Others, however, were certain that salvation was not absolute, and if one fell far enough astray, one could lose their salvation.

But there were (and are) severe problems with both these concepts. If a Christian believes in the "once saved, always saved" doctrine, it presents the danger of giving people a "license to sin." If believers' salvation is guaranteed no matter what, they could do all manner of heinous things between the first time they get saved and their death and still get to Heaven just fine.

On the other hand, if a Christian adopts a doctrine of salvation that is not absolute or somehow limited in scope, this understanding brings unforeseen consequences, as well. For example, if Christians could sin and suddenly lose their salvation, this would put them on some rather shaky ground, and no one's salvation would be guaranteed. Catholics themselves had long struggled with the idea that they could lose their salvation, and, generally, it resulted in many Catholics obsessively compulsively counting rosary beads, making the sign of the cross, and begging God for forgiveness every single time a perceived transgression occurred "lest their name be blotted out from the Book of Life."

But even if someone obsessively prays for forgiveness over every perceived offense, what if they don't have the chance to repent before dying? Furthermore, what if they committed sins that they didn't even realize were sins, such as sins of the heart? Jesus, after all, taught that to look at one's brother with hate was the same as outright killing him. Think of someone in a road rage incident screaming at a fellow motorist in full-on anger and then dying from a heart attack shortly thereafter—no chance for a sinner's prayer there. Did they lose their salvation?

Many Christians today would have a problem with the idea that the God they believe in would cast them to the side so easily. Yet, if God could look past one sin, then what about the others? Are some sins forgivable and others are not? Then again, if all sins are automatically forgiven through the finished work of the cross (as some Christians contend), what would be the point of repeatedly requesting forgiveness for something already forgiven? And, for some, this logic would seem to license all manner of unchecked sin in the knowledge that it's already forgiven anyway. As you can see, we are smack dab where we started in this rather circular argument. This, then, is the dilemma that today's theologians still struggle with.

Calvin's answer was to believe that God had predetermined it all from the very beginning. Calvinism taught that God "freely and unchangeably ordained whatsoever comes to pass." From this belief, it was determined that God had preordained some to salvation by grace, while others had been preordained to be doomed to eternal damnation for all their sins. This seems to fly in the face of 2 Peter 3:9, which says, "The Lord is not slow in keeping his promise, as some understand slowness. Instead, he is patient with you, not wanting anyone to perish, but everyone to come to repentance." If salvation was all preordained, on the other hand, then what's the point of any of it?

And many—including a former Carmelite monk by the name of Jérôme Bolsec—were keen to ask that very question. Bolsec made his way to Geneva in 1551 and actively engaged with the Calvinist movement, arguing that predestination was wrong. Jérôme argued that it was so wrong, in fact, that such belief rendered a just and holy God as the author of both good and evil. Jérôme Bolsec believed that such a treacherously unstable house of cards simply could not stand.

It was Jesus himself, after all, who refuted such a notion. According to Scripture, when unbelievers accused Christ of casting out devils through the work of devils, Christ famously stated that "if a house be divided against itself, that house cannot stand." Bolsec similarly argued that there was no way God would predetermine damnation. What was the response to Bolsec's carefully crafted argument? He was put in jail for blasphemy and heresy, and, upon his release, told to not come back.

As you can see, the sad irony all throughout the Protestant Reformation is the fact that once the previously persecuted reformers gained enough power, they in turn were ready to actively persecute others. The Calvinists, likewise, were not at all opposed to dishing out punishment to those whose beliefs they disagreed with.

Bolsec became understandably disillusioned with the Reformation after his experiences with the Calvinists—so much so that he returned to the Catholic Church. He later published a book about John Calvin in 1577 in which he blasted the reformer, calling him "a man among all others who were ever in the world ambitious, presumptuous, arrogant, cruel, malicious, vengeful, and above all ignorant." But if Bolsec thought he had been treated harshly by the Calvinists, it was nothing compared to what happened to a visiting Spaniard by the name of Miguel Servetus.

Miguel was a doctor by trade but had gotten himself into controversy by questioning the trinity, claiming that the notion was not biblical and had been completely contrived. He wrote a book that expounded upon his belief called Restitutio, which was published in 1553. Since most Protestants then believed in the trinity, Miguel managed to anger both trinity-believing Catholics and trinity-believing Protestants in just about equal measure.

Consequently, Miguel became a fugitive and was on the run when he decided to pass through Geneva, Switzerland. It was here that Miguel—now an infamous figure—was accosted by the Protestants. He was subsequently tried in Geneva for heresy, and on

October 27, 1553, he was found guilty and sentenced to be burned at the stake. Calvin, who had previously expressed his extreme revulsion to Miguel's beliefs, tried to intervene on his behalf and lessen the severity of his execution by requesting he be decapitated instead of being burned alive.

But even this courtesy was not allowed, and Miguel was burned at the stake as planned. Even though Calvin was the one showing some restraint, Miguel's death was later blamed on him. And, while some came to view Miguel as a martyr, they also began to see Calvin as a tyrant. At the theological level, another opponent to Calvin was the French thinker Sebastian Castellio, to whom all the talk about predestination, free will, angels, and the like was pointless when all that truly mattered was faith in Christ.

Sebastian Castellio argued that doctrine was imprecise, people were imperfect, and we would never be able to understand everything correctly. Having that said, Castellio contended that believers shouldn't worry so much about the correct interpretation of Scripture but simply believe as best they can, just as the "tax collectors and prostitutes" did in the New Testament. Castellio also came to the wise conclusion that there was no point in punishing heresy since no one could agree on just what might be heretical.

As Sebastian Castellio put it, "There is hardly one of all the sects, which today are without number, which does not hold the others to be heretics. So that if in one city or region you are esteemed a true believer, in the next you will be esteemed a heretic. So that if anyone today wants to live, he must have as many faiths and religions as there are cities or sects, just as a man who travels through the lands has to change his money from day to day."

Castellio, an astute and shrewd observer of what was happening around him, could see how ridiculous it was that an interpretation of Scripture that was esteemed in one city could just as easily earn one the death penalty in another. This was obviously not a sustainable model for human religious practice. Castellio had come to believe that a more general human decency was better than a zealous striving toward doctrinal correctness.

In this regard, Castellio declared, "It would be better to let a hundred, even a thousand heretics live than to put a decent man to death under pretense of heresy." Sebastian Castellio was in many ways ahead of his time with his advanced humanistic views. But as much as such statements might seem reasonable to most of us today, they provoked quite a bit of wrath in his own time. Swiss Protestants were enraged by his words—irked at the notion that he would seek to diminish biblical truth.

One Swiss reformer, Theodore de Beze, even went so far as to charge that Sebastian Castellio "advises everyone to believe whatever he wants, opening the door by this means to all heresies and false doctrines." As hard as it is for us to fathom today, many hardline Catholics and Protestants both held to their beliefs so strongly that they were willing to both die and kill for them if need be.

Calvin himself was not swayed by such arguments for religious tolerance, and in 1554 wrote up a treatise on the trinity, in which—among other things—he argued that the execution of heretics such as Miguel Servetus was completely justifiable. He continued to consolidate his power over the next few years, and in June of 1559, he established a Bible college in which his beliefs could be routinely taught in their most precise form. It was from these Calvinist missionaries that John Calvin would export his brand of the Reformation abroad.

Chapter 9 – England Rolls Back Reformation

"What made Luther's stance so outrageous was not that he valorized the Bible. That is hardly unusual for Christians. What was shocking was that he set it above everything else. He treated the views of the early church fathers, of more recent scholars, even of church councils, with great respect, but he would not be constrained by them. In the end, anything outside the Bible, including anyone else's interpretation of the Bible, was a mere opinion. This was true and enduring radicalism of Protestantism: it's readiness to question every human authority and tradition."

Alec Ryrie

After King Henry VIII passed away in January of 1547, the state of religion—or perhaps even better put, the state religion—of England had become entrenched in uncertainty. It was Henry VIII who had launched a pseudo-reformation in which he basically created his own state version of Catholicism, with himself at the head as both religious and political statesman. This meant that upon his death, this unique role would be given to his successor—the king's son, Edward VI.

King Henry's heir was only nine years old at the time of his passing, however, and was certainly not ready to perform as the sovereign political and religious monarch of England. Stepping into that role until Edward VI was ready to rule was Edward VI's uncle—also named Edward—Edward Seymour, the Duke of Somerset. The Duke of Somerset was given great power as the Lord Protector while Edward VI remained in his minority.

In the meantime, the Protestant world looked toward both King Edward VI and the Duke of Somerset with hope for future reform. Even John Calvin sent his best wishes from Geneva, telling the Duke of Somerset, "This is the age of salvation when God's word has been revealed." And these hopes were not unfounded. The earliest sign of reform came in July 1547, when the new royal government began to issue sweeping reforms in how church services were administered.

Of primary concern were traditional objects that had been largely associated with Catholicism, such as holy water, palm crosses, and the like. These were done away with, as well as many other religious icons. Along with these reformatory efforts, it was mandated that church clergy read a government-backed homily—or religious discourse—to their congregations during church services. The homily was a standard part of Catholic mass, but even though this tradition was kept, it was reformed to adhere to certain standards set by the government.

Another major change was enacted with the ending of the so-called chantries. These consisted of priests who sang and chanted prayers for the dearly departed believed to be in purgatory. Here, the Church of England had come to an agreement with many other reformers and decided that they would also disavow the concept of purgatory. It was declared that such things were not necessary and only took away from the perfect salvation through the death of Jesus Christ.

But perhaps the most important reform occurred in 1549 with the Act of Uniformity. This regulation saw to it that the Latin mass was replaced by the specially-created English-based liturgy known as the Book of Common Prayer, established by the Archbishop of Canterbury, Cranmer. This universal decree was carried out in force with the sole exception of the universities of Cambridge and Oxford, where allowances were made for scholars to still be permitted to say their prayers in the Latin tongue.

The Archbishop of Canterbury had placed a powerfully written essay inside the Book of Common Prayer, which served to set the tone for this moment in the English Reformation. The essay was called "Of Ceremonies: Why Some Be Abolished and Some Retained." As one might imagine, the subject matter covered why some of the previous religious customs had been done away with while others were kept in place. In the text, Cranmer spoke of how previous religious rituals had "blinded the people and obscured the glory of God."

It was for the sake of clarity, then, that the old ceremonial practices had to be put aside. But as much as the archbishop tried to sell the change as being for the church's own good, not everyone agreed. In the towns of Cornwall and Devon, an all-out rebellion was ignited by outraged parishioners who demanded that their old customs be restored. Known as the Western Rebellion, this episode involved infuriated churchgoers taking the prayer books and setting them ablaze.

These protesters of this seemingly homegrown Protestant Reformation then went to the administrative district of Exeter, where they made their demands known. Among them was a call to bring back Henry VIII's previous ban of English-translated Bibles. They also sought to bring back icons that were used to pray for loved ones believed to be in purgatory. They wanted to do all these things "just as [their] forefathers did."

Many of the Christian laity in these days were in the habit of reciting memorized Latin Scripture and prayers even though they did not always understand the words they were reciting. It was a pure muscle memory exercise they repeated by ear—just as their forefathers before them had done. Archbishop Cranmer took issue with this and criticized the dissidents by arguing that reciting Latin words that they did not clearly understand was no better than being a parrot.

In the end, the dissidents were only brought down by force, and after royal troops arrived from London, a violent melee ensued, killing many of the protestors. The leaders of the protest were also seized, and many of them received the death penalty for their actions. King Edward's Lord Protector, the Duke of Somerset, was having some problems of his own, meanwhile. He had been leading battles against both Scotland and France, and with the addition of having to put down insurrections at home, England was going broke.

Discontent with his leadership led to plotting against him that culminated with the Earl of Warwick taking over. The Earl of Warwick received the title of "Lord President" in the spring of 1550, and thereafter would call the shots. Soon after this power grab, Archbishop Cranmer decided to enact even more religious reform by restructuring the role of the priest. Rather than hold a primary duty of administering sacraments, the priest was made to serve more of a pastoral function and expected to focus on preaching the gospel to church members instead.

As reformative as the Book of Common Prayer was, its own author—the Archbishop of Canterbury—had begun to think that it was lacking. One of the problems was the fact that much of the previous Catholic language about mass had remained intact. Cranmer wanted to distance himself from such things, so he crafted a revised edition of the prayer book in 1552 in which he carefully removed terms such as "mass" and replaced them with "Lord's Supper" or "holy communion."

But, as is usually the case, Archbishop Cranmer still had his critics. One of his more vocal critics was John Knox, a royal chaplain who found the prayer book's admonition to kneel during communion to be unbiblical. After all, during Christ's last supper in the New Testament in which he ate and drank with the disciples—upon which communion is based—there was no one kneeling. Rather than taking the criticism seriously, however, Archbishop Cranmer refused to listen to such critiques and castigated such opponents as merely "unquiet spirits."

To further distance the Church of England from the Catholic Church, the revised prayer book also contained the Forty-Two Articles, which highlighted the main differences between the two. Specifically, Cranmer claimed that purgatory, indulgences, the veneration of images and relics, and the invocation of saints were not scriptural. The Archbishop of Canterbury denounced these Catholic beliefs and practices as "a fond thing vainly invented, and ground upon no warrant of Scripture."

But as any good Catholic knows, this is not entirely true. Both the belief of purgatory and the practice of indulgences, for example, are indeed based on Scripture. It's not something a priest simply made up out of thin air. The notions are gleaned largely from the book of Maccabees, a so-called apocryphal text that Protestants such as Martin Luther decided to omit from all Protestant copies of the Bible.

It would be one thing to disagree with the Catholic Church's interpretation of the Bible, but to say that such things are not based on Scripture is a bending of reality to suit Protestant ends. At any rate, the Archbishop of Canterbury seemed to have a free hand in both interpreting Scripture and reforming the church for a time, and for the most part did as he pleased. The momentum for reform, however, would come to a halt on July 6, 1553, when word was received that the young King Edward had passed away.

It's interesting to note that the monumental efforts that his father Henry VIII made to bring a son into this world seemingly came to naught. Henry VIII had largely broken Catholic Church tradition just to put away one wife and gain another that could bear him a son. But six wives later and an English Reformation partially underway, the main purpose of all the deceased king's efforts had perished along with him.

The death of King Edward sent shockwaves through the kingdom. But as is almost always the case in dynastic royal families, there was a back-up plan. According to Henry's will, in the event of his son's death, the crown would be handed over to Edward's eldest sister—Princess Mary. This Mary was the daughter of the Katherine of Aragon—Henry's first wife, whose marriage he had annulled and quietly put away. Ironically, Henry had left Katherine in search of a wife who would give him a son to avoid his throne being given to his and Katherine's daughter Mary. Yet, that is precisely what occurred.

Mary, who had lived through all the recent somersaults in English theology, was a diehard Catholic who very much wished to turn the clock back on England's recent Reformation. Those in government knew that this would be the case and, in a last-ditch effort, tried to thwart the queen's rise to power by backing the Protestant daughter of the Duke of Suffolk—Lady Jane Grey—instead. But as much as those who leaned Protestant rose against her, Mary successfully shored up support from those sympathetic to Catholicism.

Holed up in Framlingham Castle in Suffolk, the queen rallied her supporters around her, and in the face of her fierce support, her challengers decided to give up the fight, allowing Mary to retain the throne. Initially, Mary had hinted to her court that she intended to practice a wide-ranging religious tolerance. But soon into her reign, this proved to be more lip service than anything else. For once her power had been consolidated and assured, the queen went on a rampage. She had all Protestant preaching licenses revoked and had prominent Protestants arrested.

In this sudden role reversal, she then made sure that Catholic priests that had been imprisoned under her brother Edward VI were released and placed back in charge of their parishes. By the end of the year, all the new religious literature—including the Archbishop's Book of Common Prayer—were removed from circulation, and the traditional Catholic mass was back in place. England had seemingly reverted to Catholicism in just a matter of months.

Even more distressing to the Protestants was the news that Queen Mary was planning to marry Philip II of Spain—the son of the Holy Roman Emperor, Charles V. This marriage of political convenience had been hatched by Emperor Charles himself, who sought to wed his son with the new Catholic Queen of England to ensure both political and religious stability in the region. Fearing that their nation would become subsumed by the Holy Roman Empire due to such a union, many in the British Parliament predictably objected to the union.

It was for this reason that Queen Mary—in what was perhaps not the most eloquent of phraseology—was petitioned by the House of Commons not to wed a foreigner. Once it was clear that the queen would not be persuaded by Parliament, a noble by the name of Sir Thomas Wyatt attempted an outright coup by sending an army of some 3,000 to descend upon the queen in London. The queen's forces were more than capable of defending their monarch, however, and the army was repulsed. In the melee, Sir Thomas Wyatt was captured and summarily executed. Queen Mary was going to become the wife of Spain's King Philip whether anyone liked it or not, and the two were duly wed on July 25, 1554.

Previous reformers, such as Archbishop of Canterbury Thomas Cranmer, meanwhile were being arrested and put on trial with sudden demands for them to denounce their non-Catholic beliefs. For all intents and purposes, before the year was out, the pope was ready to welcome England back to the Roman Catholic fold with open arms. And on November 30, 1554, it was made official—England had returned to the Mother Church.

With England back in the Catholic embrace, it wasn't long before the power of the Catholic faction began to ramp up persecution of those who dared to remain Protestant. Aiding them in this was a decision by Mary's government, made in January of 1555, to implement traditional Catholic heresy laws through the old Catholic standard "On the Burning of Heretics." As the name implies, these laws gave license to the lethal punishment of any so much as accused of being heretical.

This led to several high-profile heresy trials, which amounted to nothing more than show trials reminiscent of Martin Luther's interrogation at the Diet of Worms. The main goal of such occasions was to prove Protestants to be in error while reinforcing Catholic supremacy. They also served to set examples for others lest they decide to go the same way as other supposed heretics. One of the first to be killed in this great purge was a popular London pastor by the name of John Rogers.

Rogers was burned at the stake for his refusal to submit to Catholic doctrine. Even as they lit the flames, John Rogers had steadfastly proclaimed, "That which I have preached I will seal with my blood." His death was followed by many others, and by late 1558, it's said that some 280 men and women were killed, along with countless others who simply perished while behind bars. The persecution was so bad that, at one point, even an infant who was born to a condemned woman was burned at the stake right alongside his mother.

This was apparently too much even for the most bloodthirsty of Catholic zealots, however, and the sheriff who made the fateful decision to burn the baby was ultimately charged and found guilty of homicide for the transgression. The man who had been the architect behind much of England's Protestant reform in the meantime—Archbishop Thomas Cranmer—had been arrested and kept under lock and key. In this cell, he was isolated and routinely interrogated by those who held him.

After these repeated rounds of questioning, he finally snapped and found himself signing his recantation in 1556. This led to another more formal recantation, and Cranmer officially acquiescing to papal power.

But the recantation did not last. Archbishop Cranmer was taken to Oxford University on March 21, 1556, to speak before those assembled as to why he came back to the Catholic faith. Cranmer surprised them all, however, when he began to denounce not his previous reforms but the Catholic Church and his recantation. His denunciation ended with "and as for the pope, I refuse him as Christ's enemy and false doctrine."

This was obviously not at all what the Catholic faithful wanted to hear. Once his handlers got over their shock, they immediately seized Archbishop Cranmer and proceeded to haul him off to an execution site in which he could be burned to death. It is said that while Archbishop Cranmer went up in flames, he quoted from Scripture. He repeated the words Saint Stephen had uttered while being stoned. Cranmer cried, "Lord Jesus, receive my spirit! I see the heavens open and Jesus standing at the right hand of God!"

With one of the chief architects of England's Reformation burned at the stake, it seemed that the cause for the Protestant Reformation in England was all but lost. But then, on November 17, 1558, the unexpected happened. Queen Mary died. She was only forty-two years old, but as it turns out, she had a terminal case of stomach cancer. So ended the reign of the queen who would be forever remembered as "Bloody Mary."

She was put down not by an armed overthrow from without but by cancerous tumors from within. Upon her death, Princess Elizabeth took the throne. Elizabeth was a supporter of the Reformation, and as soon as she came to power, she reversed course, broke with the Catholic Church, and began to restore the gains that had been made in England's long, drawn-out march toward religious reformation.

Chapter 10 – Huguenots, the Netherlands, and William of Orange

"In running over the pages of our history for seven hundred years, we shall scarcely find a single great event which has not promoted equality of condition. The Crusades and the English wars decimated the nobles and divided their possessions. The municipal corporations introduced democratic liberty into the bosom of feudal monarchy. The invention of fire-arms equalized the vassal and the noble on the field of battle. The art of printing opened the same resources to the minds of all classes. The post office brought knowledge alike to the door of the cottage and to the gate of the palace. And Protestantism proclaimed that all men are alike and able to find the road to heaven. The discovery of America opened a thousand new paths to fortune, and led obscure adventurers to wealth and power."

Alexis de Tocqueville

The Huguenots were Protestants who were influenced by Calvinist beliefs who took root in southwestern France in the 16th Century. Since France was officially Catholic at the time, the Huguenots had to meet in secret. They did this through a network of many Huguenot safe houses scattered throughout France. Geneva, meanwhile, remained the spiritual capital of these French reformers—and Calvinist writings were routinely smuggled into the Huguenot domain.

All this activity was, of course, vigorously rejected by French governance. In 1547, the king of France, Henri II, created a commission called "the burning chamber" specifically charged with the task of rooting out supposed heretical movements like the Huguenots. If the name doesn't give it away, the burning chamber was certainly not above killing heretics by burning them at the stake.

In fact, during the first few years of the commission, it is said that thirty-nine reformers were executed by fire or hanging. It was shortly after this purge that the Edict of Châteaubriant was issued in June of 1551. This edict enabled lower courts to have the power to carry out the execution of presumed heretics without so much as even consulting the parliamentary government.

Meanwhile over in Geneva, John Calvin—whom most Huguenots viewed as their spiritual leader, looked at these moves as nothing short of draconian. Even though Calvin also had heretics condemned, he at least gave them some semblance of a trial (although it's certainly debatable how fair they were). At any rate, for a time, France seemed to corner the market on routine execution of religious dissidents during this period.

Much of this persecution of the Huguenots was covered in Jean Crespin's 1554 text, Le Livre des Martyrs. In it, Crespin documented quite well how those punished were rounded up, tortured, and executed. To make matters even more disturbing, often the tongues of the martyrs were removed beforehand to keep them from professing their faith to the crowd. They were denied even the chance to give their last testament to those who were persecuting them.

There would be no last words—these oppressed souls had to burn in silence. In the fall of 1557, John Calvin attempted to encourage the French faithful, issuing a statement that read in part, "God desires to try our faith, like gold in the furnace—yet he fails not to treasure up their precious tears." The encouragement must have helped because, by 1559, it was clear that despite their persecution, the Huguenot movement was growing.

That spring, a group of some thirty different parishes met in France to pledge their allegiance to Calvinist doctrine. John Calvin also began to send his missionary pastors, who were trained at his Geneva Academy, to France to spread Calvinist beliefs even further. It's said that by 1564, some 100 of these Calvinist missionaries had been sent. And it seemed that all these efforts were indeed making a difference—most notably by way of the impressive rate at which members of the French upper classes began to embrace the faith.

It was amidst this renewed sympathy towards the reformers among French nobility that King Henri II unexpectedly perished during a friendly game of jousting. It was a complete accident. The elder Henri had been jousting with the younger Gabriel comte de Montgomery in celebration of his daughter's impending wedding. In their last round of jousting, Gabriel lifted his lance, charged, and accidentally struck the king head-on, causing his lance to shatter and break. It was one of the shards from his broken lance that tore through the gaps in the king's visor, slicing through the king's eye and lodging into his brain.

Interestingly, the French mystic Michel de Nostradamus has long been credited with predicting this tragedy. A few years prior, Nostradamus had published a book of vaguely-worded quatrains that allegedly predict future events, and one of them is said to have been written about this event. The quatrain stated, "The young lion will overcome the older one / On the field of combat in a single battle; He will pierce his eyes through a golden cage, / Two wounds made one, then he dies a cruel death."

Henri did indeed die a cruel death in terrible pain, perishing from the mortal wound days after the fact. In the prediction, the old lion is said to be Henri and the young lion Gabriel, who pierced Henri's eyes through his "golden cage"—in other words, pierced his eyes through his protective, cage-like visor. Nevertheless, the jury is still out on whether Nostradamus truly predicted this event or just got incredibly lucky. At any rate, it was after his death that King Henri II's successor Francois II began to renew persecution of the Huguenots.

To end the onslaught, a group of Huguenots attempted to forcibly seize the new king and hold him hostage in the spring of 1560. But their plot was found out before it could be implemented, and the plotters were apprehended. Among those who participated in the scheme were quite a few of the missionary pastors sent over from Geneva, Switzerland.

As it turns out, the plotters wasted a lot of time and energy on a problem that was on the verge of solving itself. For, in December of that very year, the young French King Francois II suddenly perished—not from the blade of an assassin, but by way of a dreadful ear infection. Upon Francois II's death, the scepter of power was handed to his brother, King Charles IX—but, since his brother was only ten years old at the time, his mother Catherine de Medici would rule in his stead until the boy king came of age.

Catherine de Medici proved to be a pragmatic politician. Sensing that her position was rather precarious, she reached out to the Huguenots to use them as a bargaining chip and wedge against the other factions arrayed against her. Also sensing that the country could not go on without some sort of compromise between the Protestants and Catholics, Catherine made a genuine effort to bridge the divide.

In furtherance of this goal, she held a summit in the fall of 1561 in which representatives of the Catholics and Protestant reformers met and openly discussed their doctrinal differences. It was a rare moment of open-minded engagement in which opposing sides could speak about their differing opinions rather than immediately slaughtering each other over them.

The meeting itself did not seem to bring much agreement, but nevertheless, in January of 1562, Huguenots were finally granted some degree of tolerance. In the Edict of St. Germain-en-Laye, it was determined that the Huguenots would be allowed to practice their faith without fear of prosecution, providing they held their gatherings outside towns, unarmed, by day, and under supervision.

Unfortunately, the toleration did not last very long at all. In March of 1562, a group of Huguenots was confronted at one of their gatherings, and the unarmed members of the flock were assaulted. The Huguenots were following the regulations as given to them— simply meeting at a barn right outside the city limits of Vassy, France—when Francis, Duke of Guise, unleashed his forces upon them. Francis later tried to claim that he did not order the attack but that it was a spontaneous violent reaction after Huguenots threw stones at his men.

At any rate, this attack left about seventy Huguenots dead and kicked off a back and forth spate of violence that would continue over the next several years. The worst eruption of this violence occurred in 1572 during the so-called St. Bartholomew's Day Massacre. The killing began on August 23, 1572, and continued for three days as militant Catholic groups systemically killed tens of thousands of Huguenots. Historians still debate the cause of the violence, whether it was spontaneous or engineered by a French official such as the Catholic Queen Catherine de Medici.

The massacre erupted following a week of festivity in France. King Charles IX was hosting the marital ceremony of Prince Henri of Navarre and his sister Margaret. Navarre was a Protestant prince, and his marriage to the Catholic Margaret was seen as a means to bring some sort of unity between Catholics and Protestants in France. Sadly, such things were not to be, and shortly after this week of feasting, the massacre occurred.

Initially, it was French troops who attacked the Huguenots, but soon Catholic civilians began to join in—literally going door to door seeking Huguenots to kill. Whatever the cause may have been, this latest Huguenot slaughter convinced many that living in France had become impossible and led to an exodus of many Huguenots to safer ground in England, Germany, and the Netherlands. Of these locales, the Netherlands would host the next major showdown between the forces of Catholicism and Protestantism.

Ever since Holy Roman Emperor Charles V had stepped down in 1556 and handed over power to his brother Ferdinand, it was agreed that direct control of what was then known as the Low Countries, or the Netherlands—which today would constitute modern-day Holland, Belgium, Luxemburg, and a piece of northern France—would fall under the dominion of the outgoing emperor's son, Philip II of Spain. Philip was too preoccupied with matters in Spain, however, and in 1559, he opted to grant his half-sister, Margaret of Parma, the authority to call the shots in this region instead.

Philip II was a staunch Catholic, but in his absence, the leading nobility of the Netherlands began to show their true colors as it pertained to support of Protestant movements and to personally back certain leaders and flocks associated with the Reformation. Philip was not too pleased by this, and as soon as he heard of it, he demanded that all supposed heresy be rooted out from the realm immediately. Nevertheless, the upper classes of the Netherlands continued to flirt with those Philip called heretics. In the meantime, a Dutch reformer by the name of Hendrik van Brederode launched the so-called League of Compromise in the fall of 1565. All of this was done to roll back restrictions that had been placed upon reformers.

When change wasn't forthcoming enough, the reformers upped the ante considerably by taking their case to Margaret of Parma. After they pressured Margaret with the specter of massive unrest unless she acted, she tried to curtail the persecution of Protestants. It was now clear that Margaret of Parma was playing a weak hand, and Protestants took advantage of it, holding massive rallies and speaking engagements in which Calvinist doctrine was freely discussed.

As was all too often the case during the Reformation, as the Protestants grew bolder, this previously persecuted group of believers soon became the ones doing the persecuting. The Protestants were against any form of religious icon or relic Catholics revered and began to strike out at Catholic Churches, tearing down paintings, sculptures, ritual implements, and the like. They also burned any Catholic literature they came across.

These Protestants wanted to be tolerated just long enough to show how intolerable they themselves could be, it seems. Their behavior shouldn't be all that surprising considering that the source of their doctrine—John Calvin—was well known for his religious intolerance. Calvin had many tortured and killed simply for having beliefs contrary to his own, as was most famously seen in the death of Miguel Servetus.

Even though it certainly wasn't a happy time for Catholics who were being assaulted and witnessing their churches demolished, it was a wonderful time for the Protestant reformers. In fact, they would later recall the year 1566 as the "Wonder Year." Margaret of Parma, meanwhile, was recalled, and the Duke of Alba was placed in charge of affairs in the Netherlands. The Duke of Alba arrived in the summer of 1567 at the head of a massive number of troops.

With the arrival of the Duke of Alba, the tables were once again decisively turned, and the persecution of Protestants began anew. The duke set up his infamous Council of Blood, in which about 10,000 were tried for heresy and at least 1,000 received the death penalty. This kicked off yet another exodus of Huguenots and other Protestants—fleeing for the high ground of German, Swiss, and English lands. In the meantime, the movement's leader, Brederode, passed away in the spring of 1568, leading to a vacuum in stewardship.

Stepping into the void was Prince William I—or, as he was more widely known, Prince William of Orange. He was called this because he controlled The Principality of Orange, which in those days consisted of part of southern France. William of Orange was a member of the Catholic nobility and had previously been neutral in the conflict, but after becoming increasingly dissatisfied with Spanish oppression of local estates and the persecution of reformers, he decided to throw in his lot with the Protestants.

William of Orange led an army against Alba's troops in 1568 but was defeated. He persisted, however, and continued a protracted kind of guerrilla warfare that would eventually lead to a major rebellion in 1572. Aiding the Protestant cause was the great discontent that Alba had created in the general population by enforcing draconian taxation on the masses. In a similar way to how Martin Luther stoked local resentment against foreign Catholic interference from Rome, William of Orange tapped into the same kind of suspicion in his subjects when it came to their Spanish Catholic overlords.

The popular uprising came to a climax when a group of pirates known as "Sea Beggars" managed to capture the port of Brill and lay siege to settlements all along the coastline. Then that August, right around the time of the infamous St. Bartholomew's Day massacre that had killed so many Huguenots in France, William of Orange took an army of tens of thousands of troops and stormed into Brabant—a part of modern-day Belgium. This assault was soon copied by several other rebel reformers.

Being attacked by both land and sea, the Duke of Alba tried to come back hard at the rebels, massacring whole towns that were in his path. His onslaught stopped the Protestants in the south, but in the northern regions, the struggle continued. It was easier to put up a resistance in the north due to both its political makeup and its geography. The north had much less of a homegrown Catholic base, and the physical terrain, with rivers and frequent flooding, was simply much more difficult for Catholic troops to invade.

Stuck in a perpetual stalemate, this long, drawn-out conflict ended up literally dividing the Netherlands along ideological lines. Ultimately, the southern region agreed to sign the Union of Arras, maintaining that they would hold fast to the Catholic Church and Spanish dominion. In the north, however, Calvinism still reigned supreme, and this led the reformers to strike up their own union, the Union of Utrecht, which was basically a pact of self-defense among the reformers in the event of foreign invasion.

By 1580, meanwhile, the Duke of Alba was out of the picture, replaced by the Duke of Parma—Alessandro Farnese. The Duke of Parma proved himself to be much more formidable in the field of battle than the Duke of Alba had been and managed to claw back Antwerp, Ghent, and Brussels from the rebels in rapid succession.

At the same time, back in Spain, Philip II made sure that William of Orange was a marked man. He castigated him as "the chief disturber of the whole state of Christendom" and extolled all good Catholics "to do him injury or take him from this world as a public enemy." Along with these words of encouragement to any would-be assassins, King Philip also placed a big bounty on the Prince of Orange, promising financial gain for anyone who was willing to take him out. The Prince of Orange was now literally a hunted man.

The first to corner their quarry was Juan de Jáuregui—a simple Spanish merchant—who came upon the prince in 1582 and managed to shoot him in both the neck and head. The Prince of Orange would miraculously survive these injuries, but it wasn't long before he faced off with another assailant hell-bent on fulfilling Philip II's directive. In July of 1584, Orange was tracked down by a lowly cabinet maker's apprentice named Balthasar Gérard.

This man managed to gain access to where the Prince of Orange was staying and then simply walked right up to him and opened fire. William was hit multiple times in the chest and abdomen. It is said that as the Prince of Orange crumpled to the ground, he shouted, "My God, have mercy on my soul!" followed by "My God, have mercy on this poor people!" Meanwhile, the assassin tried to flee, but the prince's enraged followers easily subdued him.

Gérard was not going to get away with such a brazen act and would suffer greatly for what he had done—tortured and killed by the vengeful followers of the Prince of Orange. Even though Gérard couldn't cash in on the murder, his parents were paid in full by King Philip. The death of the Prince of Orange brought immediate confusion as to how the reform movement in the Netherlands could go forward.

William of Orange's son Maurice attempted to take up the mantle of his father. Many, however, feared that it was all about to fall apart. But the reforms received some surprising aid in the summer of 1585 when Queen Elizabeth I of England sent troops to shore up the rebel reformer's strength. The queen also signed the Treaty of Nonsuch, a document that pledged intervention if the Netherlands faced invasion.

There are a few reasons why Queen Elizabeth would do this. Spain was, at this point, a political, military, and religious rival of the reformed English, and it was in the best interest of the British to have an allied (or at least neutral) Protestant buffer zone in the Netherlands. This act prevented Spanish invasion and secured the

Dutch Protestants of the Netherlands, which would eventually become the Dutch Republic, where the beliefs of the Protestant Reformation would not only be tolerated but also flourish.

The victory of the Netherlands over Catholic dominion was one of the greatest success stories of the Protestant Reformation. Many of the reformers based in the Netherlands would travel far and wide, spreading the gospel of their beliefs and way of life. Some traveled all the way to the United States of America, where they set up successful enclaves that are still in existence today.

Conclusion: How the Reformation Changed the World

When Martin Luther nailed his Ninety-five Theses to the doors of Wittenberg University, he set off a series of consequences that would have been impossible for him to have predicted. Luther had opened the door for debate, and suddenly there were protesters on every corner asking questions about why Roman Catholic doctrine was the way it was. These protesters of the religious mainstream—or, as we know them today, these Protestants—dared to hold the religious authorities of their day to task.

They wondered if purgatory was real, if faith without works would be sufficient, and if it was truly possible—or even appropriate—to pray for the dead. And when their Catholic minders failed to provide them with adequate answers to their questions, it only spurred them to ask even more. This, of course, led to the inevitable backlash of the Catholic Church persecuting the sects that arose in opposition to official Church doctrine. Unlike times past when dissidents would rise up only to be quickly cast aside, by the time Marin Luther came to prominence, these Protestants of the faith were hard for the Mother Church to shake off.

They also had a powerful tool at their disposal by way of the printing press. As Protestants printed off religious tract after religious tract, they were ensuring that their interpretation of Scripture would last long after they themselves were gone. The Catholic Church needed to come to the realization that, although they could kill the Protestant Reformers themselves, they could not kill their ideas. And as the power base of the Protestants grew, they began to govern their own cities and even countries where, for a change, they could call the shots regarding religious beliefs.

Sadly, when Protestants were finally free of persecution and able to practice as they pleased, they often turned into persecutors themselves. John Calvin, after all, burned those with differing beliefs just as fervently as the Catholics would have burned him. As much as the Reformation was an explosion of the freedom of thought and religion, it also produced dogmatic sects—so dogmatic, in fact, that each jealously guarded their form of religious expression and were willing to destroy anyone else who dared to see things from another perspective.

Although great good came from the Reformation, this was the great tragedy of the Protestants. They despised the Catholics for forcing their interpretation of Scriptures on the masses, yet they were more than ready to turn around and try to force their own heavy-handed views on others. Yes, history does indeed repeat itself, and the course of the Reformation demonstrated this phenomenon in a startling and dramatic fashion.

But, despite the perpetual back and forth rounds of persecution on both sides, much good came from the Reformation. It was the freedom of thought fostered by the Reformation, after all, that led to that other period of revolution in thinking—the Renaissance. Although the Reformation was a religious movement in nature, for many it seemed to settle some pretty serious philosophical arguments beneficial to the Renaissance.

For one thing, the Protestants defied the idea that the pope or priests had any special authority above anyone else. The Protestants took to heart Galatians 3:28, in which the Apostle Paul declared, "There is neither Jew nor Gentile, neither slave nor free, nor is there male and female, for you are all one in Christ Jesus." The acceptance of these words led to the widespread belief that all were equal under God. This leveling of the playing field worked as a bulldozer, upending the medieval belief in a natural hierarchy of authority.

Even if you didn't believe in God, the idea that everyone was equal was an eye-opening proclamation, and it was the Reformation that brought these notions directly to the masses. Protestants also encouraged innovation and a strong work ethic—all things that would find their way from Europe to a place called America. It was in America that the real fruits of the Reformation blossomed.

Free of any idea of social or religious hierarchy, the good folks of America worked hard and tried to live a good life. Following their religious precepts, they knew that hard work and a little bit of faith were all that truly mattered. The industrious free enterprise inspired by the Protestant Reformation is still bearing fruit in the United States of America to this day.

The Reformation was many things to many people, but above all, it was the seminal moment that changed the trajectory of the world for good.

Here's another book by Captivating History that you might like

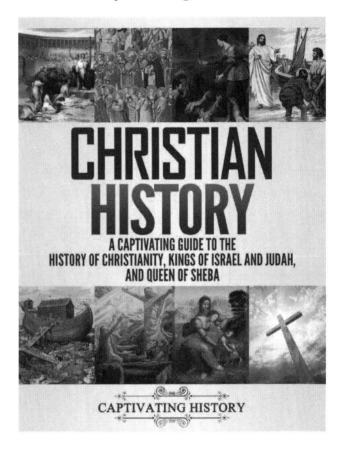

Free Bonus from Captivating History
(Available for a Limited time)

Hi History Lovers!

Now you have a chance to join our exclusive history list so you can get your first history ebook for free as well as discounts and a potential to get more history books for free! Simply visit the link below to join.

Captivatinghistory.com/ebook

Also, make sure to follow us on Facebook, Twitter and Youtube by searching for Captivating History.

Appendix A: Further Reading and Reference

Reformation: A World in Turmoil. Andrew Atherstone

The Origins and Developments of the Dutch Revolt. Graham Darby

Martin Luther: A Biography for the People. Dyron B. Daughrity

Bart D. Ehrman. *The Triumph of Christianity.* (New York: Simon & Shuster, 2008).

Tom Harpur. *The Pagan Christ.* (Toronto: Thomas Allan, 2004).

Hans Lietzmann. *A History of the Early Church*, 2 vols. (London: Lutterworth, 1967).

Philip Schaff. *History of the Christian Church*, 8 vols. (New York: Charles Scribner's sons, 1916-1923).

John D. Woodbridge and Frank James III. *Church History*, 2 vols. (Grand Rapids: Zondervan Academic, 2013).